PREFACE BY HAROLD S. WARNER III
LARRY BEAUREGARD

WALK IN THE DESTINY
YOU WERE CREATED FOR

YOU CAN BECOME A WALKING REVIVAL!

Copyright ©2023
Larry Beauregard

All rights reserved. No part of this book may be reproduced or transmitted in any form or by any means, electronic or mechanical, including recording, photocopying, or by any information storage retrieval system without permission in writing from the publisher.

Unless otherwise stated, all Scripture citation is from the New King James Version, ©1979, 1980, 1982, Thomas Nelson, Inc., Publishers.
Other versions include: GW, The God's Word Translation of the Bible, ©1995, by God's Word to the Nations. Voice, English Translation of the Bible, ©2008, 2011, by Thomas Nelson, Inc., Publishers. MSG, The Message: The Bible in Contemporary Language, ©2002, by Eugene H. Peterson. AMP, The Amplified Bible, ©1954, 1958, 1962, 1964, 1965, 1987, 2015, by Zondervan Publishing House.

Cover by: Michael N. Hauri
Edited by: Sue Maakestad
Layout by: Larry Beauregard

ISBN: 979-8-9875821-0-7

Larry Beauregard
PMB 103
2004 E. Irvington Road
Tucson, AZ 85714-1809

Printed in the United States of America

To all pastors,
congregations,
and individuals
"in Christ"
worldwide.

PREFACE

Rodney "Gypsy" Smith was a British revivalist who preached evangelistic campaigns on both sides of the Atlantic in the early decades of the 19th century. When he arrived in an area to preach at a meeting, he had a curious practice. He would stop on the outskirts of that place and draw a circle in the dirt. Then he would step inside that circle and pray, "O God, please send a revival to this town, and let it begin inside this circle."

I can vouch for the fact that ever since Larry Beauregard stepped into our little storefront adobe building in 1974, his goal was to remain inside that circle and say to God, "Let revival begin inside this circle." It's another way of saying, "Lord send revival, and let it begin in me." Hence, the term: *Walking Revival*.

To become Walking Revival requires intentionality, and Larry had that – both as a young disciple coming out of Mormonism and later as a pioneer pastor, church planter, and foreign missionary along with his wife, Susan.

God has used him in a unique fashion as he has befriended other pastors and communicated to them the heart of our vision. He has never wavered from that singular focus of being a Walking Revival.

There are pastors who faithfully feed the flock of God. We need them. There are evangelists who are gifted at stirring up the flock of God. Thank God for them.

Then there are revivalists whose focus is to revive the flock of God. This is not just someone who preaches a meeting. It is a person who eats, drinks, breathes, and sleeps revival. That is the model that I'd use to describe Larry and his ministry.

The joy is this: here we both are, fifty years later, still walking in this reality together. As you read this book, get ready to draw your own circle and step inside it.

Pastor Harold S. Warner III
Door Church – Tucson, Arizona
December 13, 2022

INTRODUCTION

In 1962, the Supreme Court deemed that the Establishment Clause prohibited the recitation of school-sponsored prayer in public schools. Thus, prayer was taken out of the public schools and my generation, the Boomers, turned on to sex, drugs, and rock-and-roll. We became the hippie generation, a powerful subculture that rejected social norms and the traditional ways of previous generations. It began as a youth movement and quickly became a revolutionary generation. We had inherited the language and countercultural values from the Beat Generation of the late '50s and early '60s. But we were set on a self-destruct mode. 1967 was the Summer of Love and the Woodstock Music Festival in 1969 was the height of the hippie movement.

As the movement began to wane, God poured His Spirit out on the hippies in what was known as the Jesus People Movement. That sovereign move of God supernaturally transitioned the hippies back into mainstream society as they began going to churches across America, wondering if the God of their parents was real. They turned to Christ by the thousands, having salvation experiences that changed their lives. By the late seventies, the Jesus People Movement also began to wane as many left the churches and gave themselves over to the American Dream. Many of the hippies had turned into Yuppies (Young Urban Professionals) and some became very successful. It was a time of great prosperity and the Name-it-and-Claim-It Prosperity Doctrine became very popular.

I had been pastoring for a few years when I became aware in the late '70s that my generation had rejected a lot about how they were raised and that spanking kids had become taboo. The Bible clearly states, "He who spares his rod hates his son, But he who loves him disciplines him promptly" (Proverbs 13:24) but this was no longer the norm. So, we raised a generation of cry-babies. As the prophet wrote: "They sow the wind, and reap the whirlwind. The stalk has no bud; it shall never produce meal. If it should produce, aliens would swallow it up" (Hosea 8:7).

What an emotional generation we have become. Social media has created an entire generation fueled by emotions and feelings. The "my truth" mentality is robbing this generation of the life it was created by God to have. But this is all fickle, at best. Like my generation, they are extremely lost. God breathed upon my generation. He needs to breathe again upon this generation, or there will be no hope.

In writing this book, my endeavor is to reveal through the Word of God what He says about life. This is His Truth, not my truth. Throw a rock in the air and it will come down. This is absolute truth that never changes. Why? Because of the law of gravity. Another absolute truth is that God loves people. "The Lord is not slack concerning His promise, as some count slackness, but is longsuffering toward us, not willing that any should perish but that all should come to repentance" (2 Peter 3:9).

Christianity is not just another philosophy; yet, in many places it is taught as one. It's not just another religion that people can pick and choose over other religions. It is a relationship: people approaching God on His terms, not their own. The truth of God revealed through Scripture – His Word, the Bible – is what He wants us to know. I have spent each chapter relaying what I believe the Bible teaches about redemption and about what a true Christan really is. It's His truth revealed by the Spirit of God.

There is a redundancy of teaching throughout this book because the truth being revealed is not taught much in churches today. You may have heard bits and pieces of it, but here I hope to put the pieces together in a way that allows you to catch the revelation that Paul the Apostle lived in his day. For years I, too, preached the bits and pieces of this revelation before I saw the pieces come together to give me an awesome glimpse of what real Christianity is all about. Catch this revelation and it will revolutionize your walk with God. Too many Christians today have a mediocre walk with God, living in unbelief and defeat most of the time. That's not how God intends for us to live.

God promised Israel that they would be a blessing to the nations as they were obedient to the covenant He made with them through Abraham. Israel would become the head or leader, not the tail. They would always be on top, having the upper hand, and never be on the bottom. As a people, they would set the standard that other nations would strive to follow. Obedience to God was essential to being exalted by God for this blessing to continue. They were blessed because God had promised. I believe this is the same place that God calls every Christian to live in. What we have from God as believers in Christ causes us also to be the head and not the tail.

> *And the LORD will make you the head and not the tail; you shall be above only, and not be beneath, if you heed the commandments of the LORD your God, which I command you today, and are careful to observe them.* **14** *So you shall not turn aside from any of the words which I command you this day, to the right or the left, to go after other gods to serve them.*
> **Deuteronomy 28:13–14**

I had been a Christian for seventeen years and a minister for fourteen years before I began to understand what I have written in this book. This is the revelation I have lived over the last 31 years of my life. It is my prayer that God will open the eyes of your understanding to this great truth of being in Christ. It requires picking up your cross daily. It requires lots of time and trials along the way to experience this truth on a daily basis – while living a life of obedience. The journey is well worth it. The phrase Walking Revival is my way of conveying this revelation: "To them God willed to make known what are the riches of the glory of this mystery among the Gentiles: which is Christ in you, the hope of glory" (Colossians 1:27).

Open your heart and lay it bare before God as you read each chapter, allowing God to speak to you. I believe He will. Our experience and knowledge of God must come from the only true source of truth in the world: the Bible, His Word. As Christians we're called to live by faith, not by feelings or emotions. Allow God's Word to become the anchor of your soul, for in this you will find true life. May God bless you in your endeavor to be all you can be in Christ Jesus our Lord. May Christ in you not only cause you to be the head and not the tail, but cause others to become attracted to you and respond to your message – that you may bear fruit, much fruit, and that your fruit remain.

Abiding in Christ is the key you becoming a Walking Revival. God desires this more than any of us ever could. That's why He came, died, and resurrected; to bring us back into a right relationship with Him, just as Adam had in the beginning. Christians are to walk in the power of the resurrected Christ within. It's an abundant life of victory. His way of building His Church and evangelizing the world is through individuals reaching individuals. God's entire Word to us is wrapped up in two commands: Love God; Love People. Simple obedience to God through these relationships will cause you to become a Walking Revival! May the Lord bless you abundantly.

Larry Beauregard
Tucson, Arizona
December 23, 2022

CONTENTS

PREFACE v
INTRODUCTION vii
FOREWORD xiii

Chapter One
WALKING 19

Chapter Two
RELATIONSHIP 49

Chapter Three
TRANSFORMATION 69

Chapter Four
SEED 81

Chapter Five
FAITH 99

Chapter Six
DISCIPLESHIP 115

Chapter Seven
CROSS 129

Chapter Eight
SUPERNATURAL 149

Chapter Nine
REALITY 171

ACKNOWLEDGMENTS 193

FOREWORD

The world's shortest complete English sentence is, "Go." It is a command often used with other words, as when Jesus said, "Go into all the world and preach the Gospel to every creature." That command was given to His first disciples and to every disciple. It is an invitation to each of us to be involved in changing the world and preparing the way for the coming of Christ. It is an invitation to be part of the greatest undertaking ever, and that undertaking involves revival.

Any pastor worth his salt is anxious to experience revival in his church or ministry. Revival is the coming alive of something that was dead. Sadly, that dead state is the case in many ministries and even in many believers – but it doesn't have to be. When Greg Ogden, author of *Discipleship and Conversion*, was asked about the state of discipleship in the Church, his one-word reply was: "superficial." The state of the Church and the state of individual believers can be remedied by applying the encouragement and promise offered in this book.

People often feel discouraged about involving themselves in ministry to souls because they think the call of God requires a great level of education or technology, or that the qualifications for ministry are too high or too nebulous or too spiritual. These well-meaning but mistaken ideas may discourage a believer from becoming a soul-winning convert of Jesus Christ. It is true that not everyone is a D. L. Moody or a William Booth, who preached to great crowds with great results. Not everyone will pastor large congregations for decades like Charles Spurgeon or D. Martyn Lloyd-Jones.

But everyone can be a "Walking Revival." Here is the practical meaning of a life lived in and for revival.

Neither Moody nor Booth started by acquiring an education. They went with what they knew. They knew that Jesus had done a miracle: He gave them a new beginning, making their lives a new creation by the power of Jesus Christ. That is what they shared from the start to the finish of their ministries. It is said that Smith Wigglesworth read only the Bible, and yet the power and influence of his ministry was worldwide. Peter, when filled with the Holy Spirit on the Day of Pentecost, had power to declare the Gospel that fear had prevented him from declaring only moments before. These two ingredients – the miracle of salvation and the filling of the Holy Spirit with the call to Go – energize the believer and are needful for any genuine ministry.

The Jesus People Movement of the '70s and '80s was a spontaneous and obvious move of God. The young people who gave their lives to Christ were excited to tell others. The common line to start up a conversation was, "Do you know God has a plan for your life?" Going from there, many were able to share the Gospel message. Their desire was to be part of a real revival. It was not some put-on excitement or a personal show, but a sincere and honest effort to respond to what had miraculously happened in their lives.

Here in these pages is a book written out of Pastor/Evangelist Larry Beauregard's personal experience. It is backed by a lifestyle fueled by his decision to be a Walking Revival: to share the Gospel with anyone he came into contact with. Whether on the job, pastoring a church, evangelizing, or simply meeting people on the streets, he got involved in their lives. I have known Larry since he and I were both pioneering churches, and I know his desire for revival and his labors to see it come to pass, both in the United States and abroad.

To be a Walking Revival is a lifestyle. It all begins with the simple and shortest command in the English language, Go. The question was and still is, Will you?

Dr. John Gooding – Pastor
Globe Christian Center
Globe, Arizona
January 2, 2023

CHAPTER ONE

WALKING

The life was the light of men.
John 1:4

GOD'S INTERVENTION

I was just minding my own business – preaching a revival in Sacramento, California – when God led me into an experience that radically changed my life in September of 1991.

Just a block off the road that we kept traveling back and forth to church every day was a barbecue restaurant. I like barbecue, so I asked the pastor if he had ever eaten there. He said he hadn't, so I suggested we have lunch there the next day.

We arrived after noon and as I walked in, I scanned the menu board on the wall. A man twenty years my senior was standing behind the counter.

"Can I help you gentlemen?" he asked. His eyes had a sense of joy and warmth about them. I was immediately drawn to this man; I was caught off guard by his demeanor.

"How's your brisket?" I asked. He quickly held up one finger.

"Just a moment," he said, turning to the cutting board to slice off a piece of brisket for me to sample. As he did, I noticed a well-worn Bible between the cash register and the end of the counter – obviously one that had been thoroughly read, time after time.

Immediately, I had a deep impression upon my spirit that said, "I'm going to show you something." Whenever I get such a deep impression, the spiritual man within comes on full alert: What is God telling me here? I knew there was something divine about this moment. God was about to reveal something to me. The man returned with a long knife in his hand and on the tip of it was a chunk of brisket.

"Try this," he said. I reached out my hand and took the piece of meat, put it in my mouth, and… it just melted with flavor, it was so tender.

"Now, you know how to do brisket!" I said.

"Yes, sir," he said, "works every time!"

"Are you a Christian?" I asked.

"The devil wouldn't think so!" he said without a moment's hesitation. I laughed. I really liked this guy. There was something beyond the ordinary that drew me in to him. I had never experienced anything like it before.

"We're both preachers," I said, gesturing to my companion. "He's a local pastor at a church not far from here and I'm an evangelist preaching a revival for him." Then we ordered.

"Go ahead and find a table and I'll bring out your food in a few minutes," he said. When he did, he asked to sit and visit with us. Everything about this guy drew me in closer. After asking a bit about the church and how long we'd been ministers, he steered the conversation to his testimony.

"I was raised in Pentecost," he said. "My mother took me to church with her almost every night as I was growing up. We would drive for hours to see one or another minister. Name any famous preacher of the 20th Century, and I've been in their meetings.

Many of them laid hands on me; some even prophesied over me; but none of that ever helped me to serve God or to live the Christian life. At last, there I was, 33 years old, with a terrible pornography problem. I would go to church on Sunday and weep before God at the altar. I wanted to be free from this. I knew it was wrong. I would cry and beg God to take the bondage away. I would be the last one to leave the altar and yet, within five minutes of arriving home, it was right back to the pornography. I was bound by it.

"One day a customer asked me what was wrong and I confided in him with great shame. Rather than condemn me, he said, 'Oh, you need to come to my church and hear my pastor teach and preach the revelation of Christ in us. That truth will set you free!' So, the following Sunday, I met him in the adult Sunday school class taught by his pastor. By the time he finished teaching – even before the morning service – I was set free from pornography! It was God's truth that set me free! I prayed at the altar with the new revelation of Christ in me, and I was truly set free. I went home and got rid of all my pornography and I was never bound by it again. I've been free ever since."

He asked us to stay a few more moments and then got up and left the table. Once again, I felt a deep impression within my spirit: "This is real Christianity." He returned with two little books in his hand, one for each of us. It was called *The Making of a Christian* by Dr. Paul G. Trulin, who was his pastor. He told us he bought the little book by the case so he could hand it out to his customers; that he knew we were Christians who loved God but that he wanted us to have the book and that he only asked that we read it. We said we would.

When I got back to the hotel room, I started to read the little book and couldn't put it down. By the time I finished it, I thought this really is real Bible Christianity. Dr. Trulin had put together all the bits and pieces of the puzzle that I had preached for years: it was the big picture. It was the 100% scripturally-based teaching of Christ in me. Once I grasped this truth, it changed my life.

God has His ways of interrupting our lives to reveal His truth. For me, it started out as just another day and my craving for a barbecued brisket sandwich. I have now spent the last 32 years of my life living out this revelation from God's Word. The remainder of this book is an outflow of that teaching at work in my life. I believe this is real Christianity. May the Lord open your eyes to this truth that will set you free and keep you free. Read on and allow God, by His Holy Spirit, to lead you into all truth and change your life. Learn what it is to become a Walking Revival, and then become one by His grace and to His glory.

JESUS CHRIST

Everywhere Jesus went, people experienced the reality of the living God. He was a Walking Revival. He didn't come to overthrow Roman rule in Israel, as the Jewish people thought the Messiah would do, even though He could have. He didn't come to start a new religion. As the fulfillment of many prophesies and promises, His life confronted man in his sinfulness. His public ministry on the earth seemed short-lived. But it was powerfully effective. All these years later, He is still having a profound effect on people everywhere.

Do you believe Jesus knew who He was? Satan knew who He was. The devil knew the real threat to him on earth was Jesus. He is in the boat with the disciples when a wind comes up. This shows the activity of Satan in nature: I've got Him on a boat and now I'm going to drown Him! But what does Jesus do? He just goes to sleep in the back of the boat. The waves on the Sea of Galilee get very high and the small boat is wildly tossed about. Jesus is sleeping but the disciples are panicking.

How could Jesus sleep in such a circumstance? Because He knew who He was. The disciples are frantic. Waves are sweeping over them and they shake Him, crying out, "Jesus, don't You care that we perish?" What did Jesus want from those disciples? He wanted them to know that nothing could happen to them as long as He was in the boat with them. There was a purpose in every move He made.

Jesus was asleep because He wanted them to know there was nothing to fear as long as He was with them. He wanted them to have faith that He would take them through the storm, not just stop the storm. In the middle of their panic and fear, Jesus held up His hand and said, "Peace, be still," and the wind had to obey. Satan wanted to destroy Jesus. But Jesus didn't fear him. He knew Satan was a defeated enemy. He knew the victory in His own heart. He knew who He was! God will to bring you to the realization that you, too, can sleep in the boat during the storm.

Supernatural things happened wherever Jesus went. Everything He did was to bring people back into a right relationship with God. As His life grows within, you will reach a position of maturity where life's emergencies will never cause you to push the panic button. What He has started in you, He's going to perfect until that day. And we know that all things work together for good to those who love God, to those who are the called according to His purpose (Romans 8:28). All things!

Jesus was beginning to move the disciples into a position of understanding and revelation. The disciples didn't see or understand the life that was in Jesus. They did not understand it on the Mount of Transfiguration. They did not understand it as they watched Him work miracles. We know this by reading the words of the disciples.

They knew about Him and He was communicating to them, but it did not break through.

Thousands of people in churches everywhere know about Jesus, but they do not know Him. They quote Scripture and read the Bible over and over, but they do not know Him. They sacrifice. They work. They serve. They confess that they have been saved. But they do not know Him. Many say they know Him; they may believe that they know Him, but they really don't.

Twenty-eight years after his conversion on the Damascus Road, Paul said in Philippians, That I may know Him (Philippians 3:10). We haven't graduated yet. We haven't arrived. We have not even entered into a fraction of knowing who He really is; yet He is within us. If God would open our eyes to see who His Son is within us to the depth that He really wants to, you and I could not contain it. Even though the disciples had walked with Him, they had not come to the life-changing revelation He was the Christ. Jesus was building upon this revelation daily. He does the same for us today. He was constantly teaching the disciples and training them, but those teachings were meant for all of us.

> When Jesus came into the region of Caesarea Philippi, He asked His disciples, saying, "Who do men say that I, the Son of Man, am?" So they said, "Some say John the Baptist, some Elijah, and others Jeremiah or one of the prophets." He said to them, "But who do you say that I am?" Simon Peter answered and said, "You are the Christ, the Son of the living God." Jesus answered and said to him, "Blessed are you, Simon Bar-Jonah, for flesh and blood has not revealed this to you, but My Father who is in heaven. And I also say to you that you are Peter, and on this rock I will build My church, and the gates of Hades shall not prevail against it. And I will give you the keys of the kingdom of heaven, and whatever you bind on earth will be bound in heaven, and whatever you loose on earth will be loosed in heaven."

> Then He commanded His disciples that they should tell no one that He was Jesus the Christ.
> **Matthew 16:13–20**

Jesus asked them the question just as He asks us today: "But who do you say that I am?" Simon Peter answered and said, "You are the Christ, the Son of the living God." Peter had revelation from the Father. What is your answer to that question? From the moment we get saved, the Father gets involved in our lives, revealing Christ to us. Then Jesus said, "Upon this rock, I will build My Church." What is the rock? Some say it is Peter. But it is not. It is the revelation of Jesus as the Christ. Jesus will build His Church upon the revelation that He is the Messiah of Scripture. When this revelation of Christ breaks through in your life, it will take all the struggles out of doing His work. It will change your entire life until you are willing to be totally spent for what you have found in this revelation of Him. Oh, that we may know Him!

Jesus then takes them further: "I'm going to give you the keys of the kingdom." Authority does not come until we have a revelation of Jesus. Here's the authority: "Whatever you bind on earth will be bound in heaven, and whatever you loose on earth will be loosed in heaven." After speaking these things concerning the Church and authority in the Kingdom of God, Jesus began stirring up everything He could to bring about His crucifixion. He went from Caesarea Philippi back to Jerusalem. He turned over the money changers' tables. He penetrated the Jewish religion until He had the whole city in an uproar and they cried, "Crucify Him! Crucify Him!" They thought that was the only way they could get rid of Him. And Matthew 16:21 says that this was exactly what He wanted: "From that time Jesus began to show to His disciples that He must go to Jerusalem, and suffer many things from the elders and chief priests and scribes, and be killed, and be raised the third day."

The biggest mistake the devil ever made was crucifying the Son of God. Where was Jesus for those three days after He said, "It is finished"? He personally invaded hell. The Light of the World walked into the darkness of fallen angels looking for the devil. He was after something He knew Satan had taken. He found Satan – not sitting on a throne, but groveling before Him, pleading. Satan knew who was before him, the only One he could not destroy. Jesus reached out and took back the authority: the keys Adam had lost back in the Garden, robbing people of everything and creating the suffering and the sorrow, the tears and the death that is in the world. Jesus reached out with that hand of the Spirit and took from Satan the keys to death, hell, and the grave. He would never have come out of the grave in His resurrected body if He had not taken those keys from Satan. When heaven's angels rolled away the stone from the tomb, Jesus stepped out of that grave. He had the keys and death was defeated. He did this for the whole world.

Spend time studying all the miracles of Jesus. Put effort into your study so that you can begin to know Him. Every miracle He performed and every parable He spoke had one purpose behind it: to bring people back into the same relationship with the living God that Adam had before he sinned. What Adam lost, Jesus restored. This is what made Jesus a Walking Revival! He was always reviving what was lost to mankind. This is where we are redeemed. As He taught at Capernaum in the synagogue, Jesus spoke some very strong truth about Himself.

> Therefore many of His disciples, when they heard this, said, "This is a hard saying; who can understand it?" When Jesus knew in Himself that His disciples complained about this, He said to them, "Does this offend you? What then if you should see the Son of Man ascend where He was before? It is the Spirit who gives life; the flesh profits nothing. The words that I speak

> to you are spirit, and they are life. But there are some of you who do not believe." For Jesus knew from the beginning who they were who did not believe, and who would betray Him. And He said, "Therefore I have said to you that no one can come to Me unless it has been granted to him by My Father." From that time many of His disciples went back and walked with Him no more. Then Jesus said to the twelve, "Do you also want to go away?" But Simon Peter answered Him, "Lord, to whom shall we go? You have the words of eternal life. Also we have come to believe and know that You are the Christ, the Son of the living God."
>
> **John 6:60–69**

The problem with many people – even in churches today – is that we try to somehow fit Jesus into our way of life and our thoughts. We want God to conform to our way of thinking and living. But Jesus saves us and changes us so that we fit into His eternal truth. This is where you will find true happiness, love, peace and hope. This is where you will find real Christianity. Every attribute of Jesus is being formed within your inner man. The center of your Christian life is Christ.

You cannot read the epistles without the realization of the indwelling Christ. God chose to communicate life to us – through His Word. The Bible is made up of words. God's Word to His creation. This is where we find eternal life, it tells us in 2 Corinthians 4:4: "whose minds the god of this age has blinded, who do not believe, lest the light of the gospel of the glory of Christ, who is the image of God, should shine on them."

We're built from within, not from without. This is what we have to learn. The world wants to mold us into its image. That's the conflict between the Christian and the world. But God wants to make you into His image. Once full surrender comes to the life that is within, your struggles begin to cease. Sometimes it's hard to die, and so we are troubled. But the more we die to self, the more Christ lives within us. Christianity is relationship, not religion. Those on the outside looking in never seem to grasp this. To them, Christianity is just another religion; another philosophy.

This is why we have to be clothed by the Word, by the nature, by the image, and by the patterns of all that Jesus is: His character; His righteousness; His purity. The nine fruits of the Spirit are images or portraits of Jesus being worked out within us. It all begins when we are born again; literally, "born from above." When Christ is born within, by faith we begin living His life daily. His death on the cross and resurrection from the dead were for our redemption; for our salvation. This is how a loving God, who created us for relationship, would bring us back into a relationship with Himself – the relationship which He had originally had with Adam. Thus, Christ within revives us back into the relationship with God that sin had once destroyed. This is what made Jesus a Walking Revival. Everywhere He went, He drew people to back to God. Reviving them – bringing them back to life! He's still doing this today.

PERSPECTIVE

I am a Walking Revival. This term can unsettle a lot of people very quickly. Upon hearing the phrase, thoughts begin going in every direction. Minds immediately try to compute what is meant by a Walking Revival. Rather than listen for a minute or two and find out what the term Walking Revival really means, they size up the person who said it and conclude that he's just arrogant and full of pride. Much like the Pharisees of old, they come to their own conclusions in order to protect their own mindsets. Paul the Apostle combated people like this on many occasions. In dealing with certain men at Corinth, he called these mindsets *strongholds*.

> For though we walk in the flesh, we do not war according to the flesh. For the weapons of our warfare are not carnal but mighty in God for pulling down strongholds, casting down arguments and every high thing that exalts itself against the knowledge of God, bringing every thought into captivity to the obedience of Christ, and being ready to punish all disobedience when your obedience is fulfilled.
> 2 Corinthians 10:3–6

Paul knew he couldn't fight and win against these strongholds in the flesh. He had weapons. They were spiritual. They were powerful. They were rooted in revelation from God's Word. They actually possessed divine power to demolish strongholds! Paul used these weapons to combat carnal men who went about deceiving those in the church at Corinth. If we are not to be deceived, we must have the same revelation Paul had in living for Christ. He was a Walking Revival because Jesus is a Walking Revival. We cannot be carnal; we must be spiritual in order to understand this term. Spiritual things happened wherever Paul went. He was involved with ordinary people in an ordinary world and was just an ordinary man called and equipped by God. He had revelation. Christ was building His Church through Paul's life and ministry. As a Walking Revival we need the mind of Christ in order for Jesus to build His Church through us.

> These things we also speak, not in words which man's wisdom teaches but which the Holy Spirit teaches, comparing spiritual things with spiritual. But the natural man does not receive the things of the Spirit of God, for they are foolishness to him; nor can he know them, because they are spiritually discerned. But he who is spiritual judges all things, yet he himself is rightly judged by no one. For "who has known the mind of the LORD that he may instruct Him?" But we have the mind of Christ.
> 1 Corinthians 2:13–16

The mind is the seat of man's rebellion against God. This is where man asserts his desire for autonomy, his longing to answer to nothing and to no one outside of himself. Paul saw the Gospel as a powerful way to infiltrate the human mind and heart. People need to be brought back to the point where they think as God thinks. When a person becomes a Christian, their whole mental frame of reference is turned upside down. At one time, they proudly pushed the sovereignty of their own opinions and wills. The unregenerate person was the supreme judge of anything moving in on their personal world. But people will never change their behavior patterns until they change the way they think. Paul wrote, "Let this mind be in you which was also in Christ Jesus" (Philippians 2:5), "And do not be conformed to this world, but be transformed by the renewing of your mind, that you may prove what is that good and acceptable and perfect will of God" (Romans 12:2).

From the moment we get saved our mind is on the pathway of being renewed. How? By the Word of God revealed through the Holy Spirit. As we grow in the grace and knowledge of our Lord Jesus Christ, living in obedience to Him, our lives daily will prove the good, acceptable and perfect will of God. This is something tangible. Others can see this as they get close to you. This happens as we grow in God and are led by the Spirit of God. You cannot live what you do not have. You cannot give what you do not possess.

I have prayed for thousands of drug addicts, alcoholics, and people bound by all kinds of things over the years and seen them instantly delivered by the power of God. They were saved. They were transformed. They were delivered. I've seen myself as somewhat of a "deliverance minister" as I see the way God has used me. But the one thing which has stood out to me more than anything else is that true deliverance doesn't just happen because something is cast out of a person or because some prayer was made and these people were instantly changed. Genuine deliverance comes by truth. It is revelation by the Spirit of God. By God's truth revealed, understood, and accepted. "Then Jesus said to those Jews who believed Him, 'If you abide in My word, you are My disciples indeed. And you shall know the truth, and the truth shall make you free'" (John 8:31–32).

To Paul, truth was everything. To those who opposed him, image was everything. The mind is like a fortress! Do you desire to bring down the fortress dominating the mind of each man and woman until Christ breaks through the walls, and the Holy Spirit enters and moves aside all resistance? Always make the case for Christ and His Gospel. Truth from God's Word is what will change strongholds. When Paul brought the Gospel to the people of Thessalonica in Acts 17:2-3, he "reasoned with them from the Scriptures, explaining and demonstrating that the Christ had to suffer and rise again from the dead."

Paul's epistles give us insight into the revelation of who we are in Christ Jesus. Being in Christ should mean everything to a genuine born again believer. Paul's teaching on living Christ daily is the key to our lives becoming a conduit for the Spirit of God to move through and touch a lost and dying world.

> How then shall they call on Him in whom they have not believed? And how shall they believe in Him of whom they have not heard? And how shall they hear without a preacher? And how shall they preach unless they are sent? As it is written: "How beautiful are the feet of those who preach the gospel of peace, Who bring glad tidings of good things!"
> **Romans 10:14–15**

The Church that Jesus is building is very real. It is supernatural. It is alive with the very breath of God. God shows up when believers gather. He's in their midst. The Church Jesus builds has never failed any generation. Man may fail. Organizations may fail. Congregations may fail. But God never fails. His promises are just as powerful today as they were the moment He revealed them.

In order to understand what being a Walking Revival is, you must be born again. We're born again into His Church, His family. We belong because of our rebirth. As a child you have everything, but you don't possess it. You have to possess your possessions. The children of Israel had Canaan, but they had to drive out the giants and displace what was there. There may be some giants in your life, but they have to be displaced, one at a time. Jesus builds His Church through believers. In all of our outreaches, missionary endeavors, and building of buildings, Jesus brings the increase and growth. It has everything to do with what God has done for us, not because of anything we've done. We depend upon God, He doesn't depend upon us.

As I look back over 45 years of ministry throughout the world, I see churches were planted and established, multitudes came to Christ, and many were baptized in the Holy Spirit. There have been so many miracles of healing and deliverance. So many testimonies. When I was younger, I told people "I did this; I did that" and the stories were real and very powerful. As I've grown older in the Lord, I can honestly look back and say, "Look what God has done." It was all His doing. He did it through me. He was able to do it through me because I was in Christ and He in me. The most I can attest to is that I obeyed. He did the rest. I am a Walking Revival because Jesus is a Walking Revival. He is building His Church through me. As you become obedient to Christ, He will build His Church through you. You, too, can become a Walking Revival. He has given us the keys of the Kingdom for this very purpose.

> I will build My church, and the gates of Hades shall not prevail against it. And I will give you the keys of the kingdom of

heaven, and whatever you bind on earth will be bound in heaven, and whatever you loose on earth will be loosed in heaven."
Matthew 16:18–19

In Galatians 2:20, Paul says, "I have been crucified with Christ; it is no longer I who live, but Christ lives in me; and the life which I now live in the flesh I live by faith in the Son of God, who loved me and gave Himself for me." One of the most powerful keys for any Christian lies in understanding and walking in the revelation of this verse. We'll come back to it over and over again, referencing it throughout this book. Paul had a great revelation here. It is the power of the cross. For us, living a victorious Christian life is directly connected to Jesus dying on the cross at Calvary. We walk by faith in who He is. We are, because He is. Through water baptism we identify with Christ in His death, burial, and resurrection. Spiritually, we're identifying with all Christ has done for us in His obedience to the will of God. When He said, "It is finished," IT IS FINISHED! There is good reason why the devil fights so much against water baptism in any culture or nation. Our identity is now found in Christ. Not in a church building. Not with a particular organization, group or denomination.

HUMILITY

No one becomes a Walking Revival without humility. This was one of Paul's spiritual weapons: "Now I, Paul, myself am pleading with you by the meekness and gentleness of Christ" (2 Corinthians 10:1). He lived his life in the humility of Christ. The more we learn of Christ, the greater our humility becomes. We in Christ. Him in us.

The Christian life is supernatural. It's not about us. It's all about Him! Christ in us! "But we have this treasure in earthen vessels, that the excellence of the power may be of God and not of us"

(2 Corinthians 4:7). Why does God put such a great treasure in such weak vessels? So the greatness of the power may be of God and not of us. Why did God choose risky, earthen vessels instead of safe, heavenly ones? Because while perfect vessels are safe, they only bring glory to themselves. Earthen vessels are risky, but they bring profound glory to God.

We all know the story of Gideon's 300. He was facing an army of 120,000 enemy soldiers. Gideon started with 32,000 soldiers.

> And the LORD said to Gideon, "The people who are with you are too many for Me to give the Midianites into their hands, lest Israel claim glory for itself against Me, saying, 'My own hand has saved me.' Now therefore, proclaim in the hearing of the people, saying, 'Whoever is fearful and afraid, let him turn and depart at once from Mount Gilead.'" And twenty-two thousand of the people returned, and ten thousand remained.
> Judges 7:2–3.

As Gideon obeyed God, the army was knocked down to 10,000 men. "But the Lord said to Gideon, 'The people are still too many; bring them down to the water, and I will test them for you there'" (Judges 7:4). God then knocked the army down to 300 men. "Then the Lord said to Gideon, 'By the three hundred men who lapped I will save you, and deliver the Midianites into your hand. Let all the other people go, every man to his place'" (Judges 7:7).

> Then he divided the three hundred men into three companies, and he put a trumpet into every man's hand, with empty pitchers, and torches inside the pitchers. And he said to them, "Look at me and do likewise; watch, and when I come to the edge of the camp you shall do as I do: When I blow the trumpet, I and all who are with me, then you also blow the trumpets on every side of the whole camp, and say, 'The sword of the LORD and of Gideon!'" So Gideon and the hundred men who were with him

> came to the outpost of the camp at the beginning of the middle watch, just as they had posted the watch; and they blew the trumpets and broke the pitchers that were in their hands. Then the three companies blew the trumpets and broke the pitchers – they held the torches in their left hands and the trumpets in their right hands for blowing – and they cried, "The sword of the LORD and of Gideon!" And every man stood in his place all around the camp; and the whole army ran and cried out and fled.
> **Judges 7:16–21**

Obedience and brokenness. The clay pots in the hands of these soldiers had to be broken in order for the light to shine forth. Like these clay pots, we need to be broken before God. That is when Christ, our treasure within, can shine forth and penetrate the darkness around us. Humility. Meekness. Jesus walked in this. We can, too.

The trumpets represent our voices, speaking for God. Like a congregation singing together in church, not every voice will sound perfect, but together it sounds heavenly. Our witness is Christ in us. I doubt these 300 men were world-renowned musicians. They may have sounded terrible. Though not perfect, we can rest in God and He will move through us as we live Christ daily. He works through us. He works with us.

> Come to Me, all you who labor and are heavy laden, and I will give you rest. Take My yoke upon you and learn from Me, for I am gentle and lowly in heart, and you will find rest for your souls. For My yoke is easy and My burden is light."
> **Matthew 11:28–30**

Christ in us is a precious and priceless treasure. God's presence is deposited into earthly vessels. We are so worthless and weak, corruptible and perishable. Yet, imagine – Christ Himself is placed into such earthly bodies! We find rest in Christ. As we surrender to

Him, we begin realizing the Christian life is not quite as burdensome as we thought in the beginning. Some Christians have lived with their spirits so heavy for so long, that if they felt good, they would feel guilty. God never intended you to live with a heavy spirit. God never intended for you to live overburdened by your circumstances. The more we are yoked to Christ, the easier it is to serve God. Often, we look back and beat ourselves up because we didn't do this or didn't do that. But we did the best we could at that time. The devil always tries to beat us up over yesterday's failures. These are the things we have to learn to lay on the altar and let God work them out.

My desire is to see you lifted out of the place of condemnation. Lifted out of the place of questioning. Lifted out of the place of insecurity. Lifted out of the place of wondering if God really loves you and into the place of knowing who you are in Christ! Many judge their position by the many problems they face in life. We need to get to that place of really knowing who we are in Christ! It is God who has brought you into the realization of your identity in Him. You do not get here by emotions and feelings. Don't be deceived. You get here by truth revealed and obeyed. The presence of God in our hearts and bodies is power! It is the power to convert and transform us into new creatures, as it says in 2 Corinthians 5:17, "Therefore if any man be in Christ, he is a new creature: old things are passed away; Behold, all things are become new."

You no longer have to be a victim of the past! It is His divine nature in you! You're the same person but you're not the same. God gives you life, both abundant and eternal! Jesus said, "The thief does not come except to steal, and to kill, and to destroy. I have come that they may have life, and that they may have it more abundantly"

(John 10:10). Only Christ Himself, our glorious treasure, can enter our lives and change us. It is poured into our clay pitchers – the glorious treasure of Christ living within the believer – by the power of God's Holy Spirit. The Christian life is not ours because of something we do. It is who we are in Christ.

A DECEIVED GENERATION

The Bible tells us, "Let God be true but every man a liar" (Romans 3:3). Truth is truth in every generation since the beginning of man. God's truth never changes because God never changes. Every one of us has a sin nature. That never changes, either. God's truth has stood the test of time. The Bible is God's everlasting truth revealed to us. You want real truth? Go to the Bible. You will not find real truth anywhere else. God gave us His Word. As Christians, we live His truth daily. We live by faith, not by feelings.

Today's generation, for the most part, is controlled by its emotions and feelings. This control has become more acute because social media tells people that whatever they feel about something becomes "their truth" about it. It is not absolute truth, but only a lie they believe and embrace at the moment. Emotions are constantly being stirred up – tossed to and fro like the waves of a raging sea as these two things control their lives: feelings and emotions. Rational, logical thought usually doesn't fit into the narrative here. Feelings and emotions are prime fodder for deception.

Deception will be prevalent before Christ's soon return. Concerning the last days, Jesus said, "Take heed that no one deceives you" (Matthew 24:4). He then said, "For false christs and false prophets will rise and show great signs and wonders to deceive, if possible, even the elect" (Matthew 24:24). Deception will be so strong that even believers can be deceived if not properly rooted and grounded in God's Word. When the Sadducees questioned Him about the resurrection in Mark 12:24 Jesus said, "Are you not therefore mistaken [deceived] because you do not know the Scriptures nor the power of God?" Paul wrote, "For sin, taking occasion by the commandment, deceived me, and by it killed me" (Romans 7:11). The law helps convict the sinner of his guilt. It enforces the wrong of our sinful deeds. It helps to persuade the soul of its evil. Paul says, "I was alive in thinking my sin was acceptable, but then came the commandment [the Law] and the sinfulness of my sin was exposed and I was convicted, realizing instead of life and seeing myself as good, sin was wrong and was giving me death."

> Do you not know that the unrighteous will not inherit the kingdom of God? Do not be deceived. Neither fornicators, nor idolaters, nor adulterers, nor homosexuals, nor sodomites, nor thieves, nor covetous, nor drunkards, nor revilers, nor extortioners will inherit the kingdom of God. And such were some of you.
> **1 Corinthians 6:9–11**

The fact that people can be deceived is well documented in Scripture. Paul also tells us in Galatians 6:7: "Do not be deceived, God is not mocked; for whatever a man sows, that he will also reap," and in 2 Thessalonians 2:11-12, "And for this reason God will send them strong delusion, that they should believe the lie, 12 that they all may be condemned who did not believe the truth but had pleasure in unrighteousness."

> But evil men and impostors will grow worse and worse, deceiving and being deceived. But you must continue in the things which you have learned and been assured of, knowing from whom you have learned them, and that from childhood you

> have known the Holy Scriptures, which are able to make you wise for salvation through faith which is in Christ Jesus.
> **2 Timothy 3:13–15**

> For we ourselves were also once foolish, disobedient, deceived, serving various lusts and pleasures, living in malice and envy, hateful and hating one another.
> **Titus 3:3**

> But even if our gospel is veiled, it is veiled to those who are perishing, whose minds the god of this age has blinded, who do not believe, lest the light of the gospel of the glory of Christ, who is the image of God, should shine on them.
> **2 Corinthians 4:3–4**

Without Christ in a person's life, they are wide open to being deceived. They are blinded by the god of this age.

> In whom the god of this world hath blinded the minds of them which believe not, lest the light of the glorious gospel of Christ, who is the image of God, should shine unto them.
> **2 Corinthians 4:4**

> Grace to you and peace from God the Father and our Lord Jesus Christ, who gave Himself for our sins, that He might deliver us from this present evil age, according to the will of our God and Father, to whom be glory forever and ever. Amen.
> **Galatians 1:3–5**

The only way to escape deception is to know God and to know His Word. Jesus said, "It is written, 'Man shall not live by bread alone, but by every word that proceeds from the mouth of God'" (Matthew 4:4). Having received Christ in your life, walk in Him.

> As you therefore have received Christ Jesus the Lord, so walk in Him, rooted and built up in Him and established in the faith, as you have been taught, abounding in it with thanksgiving. Beware lest anyone cheat you through philosophy and empty

> deceit, according to the tradition of men, according to the basic principles of the world, and not according to Christ. For in Him dwells all the fullness of the Godhead bodily; and you are complete in Him, who is the head of all principality and power.
> **Colossians 2:6–10**

When you live Christ you live truth. Something begins growing within until you know. You know He's just as great when you feel bad as when you feel good. You don't move in the wilderness of emotions. You're not overwhelmed by feelings of frustration. God isn't like the tides of the sea. He doesn't come and go, here today and gone tomorrow. The life of Christ inside of you continues to swallow up all the patterns from your past and the desires of your appetites. There are passions that have been inflamed by sin, but He takes the fire out. Everything inside of you was made for His purposes, but sin inflamed it until you became a vehicle of darkness, unrighteousness, and evil.

When Jesus comes in, He begins taking all these things out and begins bringing your whole lifestyle back into the divine pattern where it belongs. This is truth. Peter describes it this way:

> But ye are a chosen generation, a royal priesthood, an holy nation, a peculiar people; that ye should shew forth the praises of him who hath called you out of darkness into his marvellous light:
> **1 Peter 2:9**

WARFARE

Building His Church involves warfare. God is more aware of this fight than we are. He is there for us every step of the way. Paul understood the real battle. All warfare is spiritual. He learned to fight battles by the Spirit, and not by the flesh. That's why he was a winner no matter what he faced in life. Paul understood this warfare well:

> For we do not wrestle against flesh and blood, but against principalities, against powers, against the rulers of the darkness of this age, against spiritual hosts of wickedness in the heavenly places.
> **Ephesians 6:12**

Spiritual warfare is primarily about bringing truth to bear upon people's minds. There is always the spiritual behind the physical. In reality, we are not fighting against people. Matthew 16:18 is where Jesus first revealed the building of His Church. He said, "I will build My church, and the gates of Hades shall not prevail against it." He continues to build His Church to this day. But there is warfare. Lots of warfare. Gates are the weakest point in a wall. They prevent people from going in or coming out. Gates never launch an attack. They withstand attacks. Gates are a place of control and power. It was usually at the gates where the seat of power was located in a city. Abraham's nephew Lot was seated at these gates when the two angels came to Sodom.

Hades is the realm of the dead. The gates of Hades probably symbolize entrance into that realm. Some scholars believe the Lord was declaring that death will never triumph over His Church. That could be. But sticking to the context in Matthew 16 and in light of other Scripture, let's take another look at this. One fact that never changes is that every person born into this world has a sin nature. We are all corrupt, defiled from within, unclean, evil, and unrighteous. We're all dead to God in trespasses and sin. This is the mindset or stronghold of every person without Christ. People are lost to God because of sin. All are under the judgement of death because of sin. Paul writes, "There is none righteous, no, not one" (Romans 3:10), and again, "For all have sinned and fall short of the glory of God" (Romans 3:23). In Ephesians, he breaks it down even further and says:

> And you He made alive, who were dead in trespasses and sins, in which you once walked according to the course of this world, according to the prince of the power of the air, the spirit who now works in the sons of disobedience, among whom also we all once conducted ourselves in the lusts of our flesh, fulfilling the desires of the flesh and of the mind, and were by nature children of wrath, just as the others.
> **Ephesians 2:1–3**

Being dead in sin means we're living the stronghold of a sinner. Everything about our thinking, living, and morals is in opposition to God. Until Christ is born within, we're facing certain judgment by the wrath of God. No one born into this world is exempt from this sentence of death. Romans 6:17 says, "But God be thanked that though you were slaves of sin, yet you obeyed from the heart that form of doctrine to which you were delivered." Three steps are made evident in this scripture. First, the Gospel of Jesus Christ affects the mind: our understanding. Then it moves to the heart, and we believe. Then we exercise our will: we obey. Paul finishes his thoughts, "For the wages of sin is death, but the gift of God is eternal life in Christ Jesus our Lord" (Romans 6:23). Salvation is a gift from God. You cannot earn it. It simply needs to be received. Everything else begins to flow from that.

As a Walking Revival, you will face all kinds of warfare as you reach out to the lost. Bearing witness the revelation that Jesus is the Christ is declaring war on the stronghold of the sinner. They will fight back. They will stand their ground. They will resist. It takes a supernatural moving of the Holy Spirit of God to convict them.

> Nevertheless I tell you the truth. It is to your advantage that I go away; for if I do not go away, the Helper will not come to you; but if I depart, I will send Him to you. And when He has come, He will convict the world of sin, and of righteousness, and of judgment: of sin, because they do not believe in Me; of

righteousness, because I go to My Father and you see Me no more; of judgment, because the ruler of this world is judged.
John 16:7–11

When conviction comes to the sinner, they become aware of their need of a Savior. Their heart and mind are softened and become open to responding to the living Christ. Satan is at war with God. People, the crown of God's creation, are his target; the human mind is the battleground. There is much warfare involved in reaching the lost, and even more warfare after they've received Christ as their Savior and are born into the household of faith, the Church.

Jesus opened up to the disciples about His purpose on the earth: He was building His Church. It is a community of believers. When you're born again, you're born into the family of God. In a sense you become a new form of humanity. Believers. Everything within God's kingdom moves by faith. You begin gathering with other believers and, as you gather, you become the Church. Man does not own the Church. God does.

As you study the great revivals of the past two thousand years, you begin to realize they all came about because the Holy Spirit began moving amongst a people, convicting them of sin, of righteousness, and of judgment. It is supernatural. It is God's doing. He is reaching out to them through us. The dead in sin have walls surrounding their minds; strongholds. But there are gates in the wall. These gates are at the seat of their power. But these gates shall not prevail in stopping the witness of Christ from breaking through all their defenses and bringing them to the saving knowledge of Jesus Christ. As we move by the Spirit of God, testifying as to who Christ is, this revelation is like a battering ram against those gates. This heaven-sent, Holy Spirit witness brings conviction to the sinner, convincing them of their need for Jesus Christ as Savior. This Holy

Spirit conviction causes godly sorrow. Godly sorrow brings about repentance. Repentance brings about salvation. Whatever walls the devil has set up as the stronghold controlling the sinner, this witness of Christ breaks through the gates holding the power of the stronghold and reaches out to the dead in sin to bring forth life! It takes the Holy Spirit of God moving through us to reach the sinner. This is how Jesus set things up to build His Church. He has partnered with us, the redeemed. From the moment we are saved, we become co-laborers with Him.

But there is warfare involved in the building of His Church. From the moment the Gospel of Matthew was written, the devil began to war against the truth it proclaimed. We've had two centuries of debate on whether the Church is built upon Peter or Jesus. So quickly, the devil moves to thwart the truth of Christ! As I mentioned before, the real battle is over the souls of people. The Church that Jesus is building is always triumphant! It is on the move and it is never defeated because Christ is never defeated. The devil and his strongholds are trying to hold out against the move of God in His Church. But the devil was defeated by God through Jesus Christ once and for all, and his strongholds will not prevail! It is the Church Triumphant that Jesus is building. Read these next portions of Scripture slowly and take in God's revelation to us. I know they're a bit lengthy, but they are well worth the time spent in reading. This has everything to do with our being a Walking Revival.

> He is the image of the invisible God, the firstborn over all creation. For by Him all things were created that are in heaven and that are on earth, visible and invisible, whether thrones or dominions or principalities or powers. All things were created through Him and for Him. And He is before all things, and in Him all things consist. And He is the head of the body, the

church, who is the beginning, the firstborn from the dead, that in all things He may have the preeminence.
Colossians 1:15–18

And you, being dead in your trespasses and the uncircumcision of your flesh, He has made alive together with Him, having forgiven you all trespasses, having wiped out the handwriting of requirements that was against us, which was contrary to us. And He has taken it out of the way, having nailed it to the cross. Having disarmed principalities and powers, He made a public spectacle of them, triumphing over them in it.
Colossians 2:13–15

Therefore I also, after I heard of your faith in the Lord Jesus and your love for all the saints, do not cease to give thanks for you, making mention of you in my prayers: that the God of our Lord Jesus Christ, the Father of glory, may give to you the spirit of wisdom and revelation in the knowledge of Him, the eyes of your understanding being enlightened; that you may know what is the hope of His calling, what are the riches of the glory of His inheritance in the saints, and what is the exceeding greatness of His power toward us who believe, according to the working of His mighty power which He worked in Christ when He raised Him from the dead and seated Him at His right hand in the heavenly places, far above all principality and power and might and dominion, and every name that is named, not only in this age but also in that which is to come. And He put all things under His feet, and gave Him to be head over all things to the church, which is His body, the fullness of Him who fills all in all.
Ephesians 1:15–23

The moment Jesus told the disciples the truth about building His Church, the warfare began. And it was close to home. The devil wasted no time here. Look at Matthew 16 with me one more time:

From that time Jesus began to show to His disciples that He must go to Jerusalem, and suffer many things from the elders and chief priests and scribes, and be killed, and be raised the third day. Then Peter took Him aside and began to rebuke Him,

> saying, "Far be it from You, Lord; this shall not happen to You!" But He turned and said to Peter, "Get behind Me, Satan! You are an offense to Me, for you are not mindful of the things of God, but the things of men."
> **Matthew 16:21–23**

I'll never forget the day that I read this and all at once, it hit me that Jesus did not address Peter, even though He was speaking to him. He addressed Satan. This is the warfare I'm talking about. Jesus reveals His will in building the Church, and there is nothing the devil can do to stop this. Jesus then began telling the disciples what He was going to go through in the will of God in order to build His Church.

Out of Peter, the disciple of Jesus, Satan spoke his will. Here you have God's will pitted against the devil's will. This takes you right back to the Garden of Eden when the will of God said, "Don't eat the fruit of this tree," and Satan, questioning God's will with his will said, "Yea, Has God said?" This is where the real fight takes place. It is spiritual.

Peter had been as close to Jesus as any other disciple, but Satan was still able to use him against Jesus to push his will; his agenda. Jesus said, "This is what is going to happen." Then Peter said, "Not so, Lord." God's will against Satan's will. The fight was on. Peter felt he was right in saying this. The thought just popped into his mind and he spoke it out. That's the flesh. Satan will operate through the flesh every chance he gets. But Jesus was always on guard and was listening with His spirit. He was ready for this. The words of Peter packed a spiritual punch that normal words don't. To the other disciples, what Peter said was probably what they themselves were also thinking. They all had a lot of growing up ahead of them. But as it is with all believers, not every thought passing through the disciples' minds was their own thought. Oh, the subtlety of Satan's warfare against Jesus!

Jesus felt those words, not as coming from Peter, but from the darkness of Satan's will being imposed upon Him. Jesus didn't address Peter who had spoken those words, but Satan who had planted them in Peter's spirit. By doing this, He broke the power of those words. It would be far easier for Jesus to surrender one last time to God's will in Gethsemane without those words out of Peter's mouth still packing a punch. That's why He confronted its source right on the spot. By doing this, He killed the power of that punch. There is depth to this warfare. Paul understood this.

> I say then: Walk in the Spirit, and you shall not fulfill the lust of the flesh. For the flesh lusts against the Spirit, and the Spirit against the flesh; and these are contrary to one another, so that you do not do the things that you wish.
> **Galatians 5:16–17**

From the moment we get saved, we begin to grow in God. But not without a fight. There is a fight involved as we grow in Christ. Satan doesn't just sit back and say, "Well, here we go again. Oh, well: I've just lost another one." You might have resisted the Gospel many times just like Saul of Tarsus did. But the testimony of Christ kept moving against the gates of strongholds that had you bound. Those gates could not prevail against the testimony of Christ. Eventually, they were busted through, and the conviction of the Spirit of God began to prevail. Then you repented and got saved. From the moment of your salvation experience, Satan is right there to fight back.

As soon as the king of Sodom was defeated by Abraham, he immediately spoke about the spoils of the war in Genesis 14:21: "Now the king of Sodom said to Abram, 'Give me the persons [souls], and take the goods for yourself.'" This reveals what Satan is really after and what the war is really all about. The moment we bow our knee to Jesus, we enter this war. As we put our faith in Christ and live for Him daily, we will grow. Every testing and trial we go through is for a reason. Our obedience to Christ tears down the strongholds that have bound us throughout our life. As we grow in God, our lives are increasingly more of Jesus and less of us. This is what can make us a Walking Revival. The more of Jesus moving through us, the greater influence we will have in reaching the lost, and Jesus will build His Church through us. This is the Christian life! Jesus was no ordinary man. He was the Son of God who died on the cross for our sins and was raised again triumphant. He is a Walking Revival.

> God, who at various times and in various ways spoke in time past to the fathers by the prophets, has in these last days spoken to us by His Son, whom He has appointed heir of all things, through whom also He made the worlds; who being the brightness of His glory and the express image of His person, and upholding all things by the word of His power, when He had by Himself purged our sins, sat down at the right hand of the Majesty on high, having become so much better than the angels, as He has by inheritance obtained a more excellent name than they.
> **Hebrews 1:1–4**

is pride and rebellion. And sin will always sever relationships which were at one time good. Jesus told the disciples, "I saw Satan fall like lightning from heaven" (Luke 10:18).

The judgment of God was certain and swift. Lucifer was immediately cast down to planet Earth and became "the god of this world" (2 Corinthians 4:4). Here he and his fallen angels lived out their delusion, feeling free from God's control. Lucifer ruled. All was chaos and darkness. Then God spoke, bringing light and order to His creation. Setting boundaries. Creating new things. He spoke and creation obeyed. Over six days, God brought all chaos into order and there was nothing Lucifer could do to stop it. Lucifer and his angels adjusted to the changes God made to their domain. They could live with it – until the sixth day when God created man. This they could not live with! This was beyond their comprehension. They were infuriated.

Genesis 2:7 says, "And the Lord God formed man of the dust of the ground, and breathed into his nostrils the breath of life; and man became a living being." The breath of life came from God, causing the dust to breathe, to live. Adam was created in God's image. He was created with sovereignty: a will to choose right from wrong; good from evil. He had a mind to think things through; to come to conclusions. He had logic. He had choice. But more than that: He had relationship with the living God and there was nothing Lucifer or his demons could do about it. They couldn't touch him. Adam had something they had lost: relationship with God.

It was as perfect a world as could ever be. Man was created for fellowship with God; to have relationship with Him. Because man was created with a choice between good and evil – knowing right from wrong – these opposites had to exist. He had to have choice. God gave Adam that choice in one thing: whether to eat the fruit of the

Tree of the Knowledge of Good and Evil. How simple life was then. This was the tree that was in the middle of the Garden of Eden, surrounded by the whole garden. Possibly, this was the designated spot where God met with Adam daily; where they built relationship. From the moment of his creation, Adam enjoyed that relationship – and so did God. Adam wasn't created to be a robot, programmed only to obey. He was created to have relationship with God. This relationship was rooted in the free choice that Adam had been created with. Life was great! Adam was smart. I'm sure he conferred with God daily about names for the animals and plants. Relationship. This went on for some time before Adam realized his loneliness for someone of his own kind. It was now time for God to create for Adam "a help meet" – a perfect fit. But rather than being created from above, as Adam was, Eve was created from below, from Adam's side. She was created out of God's creation. In Genesis 2:23, Adam said, "This is now bone of my bones and flesh of my flesh; she shall be called Woman, because she was taken out of Man."

HORIZONTAL

Now the serpent was more cunning than any beast of the field which the Lord God had made. And he said to the woman, "Has God indeed said, 'You shall not eat of every tree of the garden'?" And the woman said to the serpent, "We may eat the fruit of the trees of the garden; but of the fruit of the tree which is in the midst of the garden, God has said, 'You shall not eat it, nor shall you touch it, lest you die.'" Then the serpent said to the woman, "You will not surely die. For God knows that in the day you eat of it your eyes will be opened, and you will be like God, knowing good and evil." So when the woman saw that the tree was good for food, that it was pleasant to the eyes, and a tree desirable to make one wise, she took of its fruit and ate. She also gave to her husband with her, and he ate. Then the eyes of both of them were opened, and they knew that they were naked; and they sewed fig leaves together and made themselves coverings. And they heard the sound of the Lord God walking in the garden in the cool of the day, and Adam and his wife hid themselves from the presence of the Lord God among the trees of the garden. Then the Lord God called to Adam and said to him, "Where are you?" So he said, "I heard Your voice in the garden, and I was afraid because I was naked; and I hid myself." And He said, "Who told you that you were naked? Have you eaten from the tree of which I commanded you that you should not eat?" Then the man said, "The woman whom You gave to be with me, she gave me of the tree, and I ate." And the Lord God said to the woman, "What is this you have done?" The woman said, "The serpent deceived me, and I ate."

Genesis 3:1-13

The first strategy of the enemy of our souls was to sever the relationship between God and man. Somehow the devil had to drive a wedge between them. The first real battlefield God's creation ever encountered was the battlefield of trust. Look again at Genesis 3:1: "Now the serpent was more cunning than any beast of the field which the Lord God had made. And he said to the woman, "Has God indeed said, 'you shall not eat of every tree of the garden'?"

In his cunning, the devil caused Eve to question the truthfulness of God and His Word. As she allowed her mind to dwell on these new thoughts about God, she eventually began to question His trustworthiness. She began to question the will of God now, as another will was imposed upon her thinking. Once the thought was planted in her mind, it had power. Suddenly, there was war within her spirit. For the first time in her life, she had two ways to think; two ways to go. I'm sure she faced confusion. I'm sure she even spoke with Adam about the conflict within. As he listened to her, the power of that other will began working on him, as well. It didn't have the same power, but it did have power nonetheless.

Adam probably cautioned Eve on her thinking. But she couldn't let it go. The thought had power because it was imparted from another realm, another kingdom. A kingdom at war with God Himself. In planting this thought of distrust in Eve, and causing her to dwell on it, the devil began driving a wedge between Adam and Eve – thus, driving a wedge between Adam, Eve, and God. Even though the thoughts were spiritual in nature, they were played out in carnal appetites, as we read in Genesis 3:6, "So when the woman saw that the tree was good for food, that it was pleasant to the eyes, and a tree desirable to make one wise, she took of its fruit and ate."

Here began the war of flesh versus spirit. The more Eve flirted with the idea of eating the fruit – contemplating its effects on her personally – the less she trusted God and His Word. The more she gave in to those ideas, the deeper the wedge was driven between her and her husband; between both of them and God. The moment she ate of the fruit, something about her changed, exciting Adam as he'd never felt before. He had to make a decision. Would he or would he not eat of the fruit? Not eating it would sever the relationship with his wife. The lure of the flesh was overwhelming. Something about her demeanor moved him in a way that he didn't want to lose her. The flesh versus the spirit. The decision to eat or not eat of the fruit came down to relationship. Should he continue his relationship with Eve in her disobedience (flesh) or refuse to follow her example and preserve his relationship with God (spirit)? He had to decide. Adam had never experienced anything like this before. His desire wasn't for the fruit. His desire was to please Eve. He allowed his desire in pleasing her to interfere with his obedience to God. Adam allowed himself to be enticed by Eve into disobeying God, thus severing his relationship with Him.

> But each one is tempted when he is drawn away by his own desires and enticed.
> **James 1:14**

so, has placed millions of people into bondage, worshipping a false god. It will get them nowhere in the afterlife.

In the beginning God created the heavens and the earth. He created the heavens first and then He created the earth. In creating the heavens, He created angels. Created into these angelic beings is a hierarchy. A chain of command. The highest of all created intelligences was Lucifer, the morning star, "the anointed cherub" (Ezekiel 28:14). He had relationship with the living God. Even the government of God's rule passed through Lucifer, the highest of created beings at the time. Delegation of authority passed through him to other angelic beings. Because of his exalted position, somewhere along the line, he became corrupted. He was in love with himself and his own power (which had only been given him by God). He became puffed up within himself because of pride and began seeing himself as higher than God, and deluded himself into thinking he could become God, or take the place of God.

> "How you are fallen from heaven, O Lucifer, son of the morning! How you are cut down to the ground, You who weakened the nations! For you have said in your heart: 'I will ascend into heaven, I will exalt my throne above the stars of God; I will also sit on the mount of the congregation On the farthest sides of the north; I will ascend above the heights of the clouds, I will be like the Most High.' Yet you shall be brought down to Sheol, To the lowest depths of the Pit."
> **Isaiah 14:12-15**

Lucifer rebelled against God. His rebellion severed the relationship he had enjoyed for so long with God. Now he was a twisted, deluded being. In the workings of his demented mind, he plotted to overthrow God and was able to sway one third of the angels into following him in his rebellion. They had their own agenda for rebelling against God and the other angels. At the root of all sin

CHAPTER TWO

RELATIONSHIP

God was in Christ reconciling the world to Himself.
2 Corinthians 5:19

VERTICAL

In order to further understand what a Walking Revival really is, we need to understand relationship. "In the beginning God created the heavens and the earth" (Genesis 1:1). This is a statement. An absolute. A declaration. The basis of all truth. In fact, miss this one truth and you have no truth at all. This one opening sentence of the Bible demands as true the very existence of God! In the beginning God… This tells us He was before the beginning; He is eternal. This is the foundational truth of all reality. It's not "my truth" but real truth! Truth that is truth in any culture. Truth that stands throughout time and eternity! God was there before time began and even before the universe began. He created it all! He spoke it into existence! He created something out of nothing! The living God is the only Creator. There are no others. The universe has design. It was thought. Then it was created. No finite being possesses the power to create something out of nothing. Only He can and He did! The revered cow in India is worshipped as a god. But the cow doesn't even know she is considered a god. No cow has ever created anything! Religion has placed this lie upon the cow and, by doing

> Then to Adam He said, "Because you have heeded the voice of your wife, and have eaten from the tree of which I commanded you, saying, 'You shall not eat of it': "Cursed is the ground for your sake; in toil you shall eat of it all the days of your life."
> **Genesis 3:17**

THE FALL

Lucifer sought to overthrow man's sovereignty. He influenced their will to choose. God said they would die. They didn't immediately die physically. But this one thing we know for sure: they died spiritually. Relationship was broken. Dominion in the earth was lost. The sin nature was born. God was coming to meet with them, and the first thing they did was hide. Then they tried pointing the finger at others for the severed relationship. It's always someone else's fault. As sinners we point the finger at anyone but ourselves. From that moment on, every child born would have that sin nature. Sin separates and divides. "All have sinned and come short of the glory of God" (Romans 3:23). They clothe themselves in leaves, but God clothes them in animal skins. Redemption. His plan. The innocent dies for the guilty to cover sin.

Now that sin has entered, the devil can influence people. Control them. Without a relationship with the living God, the devil becomes the chief influencer in people's lives and we are now under the influence of the god of this world. Without relationship with God we have no dominion. Sin controls us. We live as slaves to sin, as Jesus said in John 8:34: "Most assuredly, I say to you, whoever commits sin is a slave of sin."

We are all sinners by nature. We are not sinners because we sin. We sin because we are sinners. We're born with the sin nature. Because of the sin nature we're separated from God. Being separated from God means our relationship with Him is broken. It doesn't exist.

The entire Kingdom of God is relationships. Relationship with God (vertical) and relationship with one another (horizontal). Love is foundational to all relationships.

> Jesus said to him, " 'You shall love the LORD your God with all your heart, with all your soul, and with all your mind.' This is the first and great commandment. And the second is like it: 'You shall love your neighbor as yourself.' On these two commandments hang all the Law and the Prophets."
> **Matthew 22:37-40**

Everything concerning the Kingdom of God has to do with relationships. Jesus takes all the teaching of the Old Testament, all of Jewish history, and breaks it down into two categories: Love God; Love People. Relationships.

A NEW NATURE

Christianity is not a doctrine or a belief. It is an exchanged life. You're born with a death nature through Adam, but Jesus came to give you new life through a new nature. He came to give you what you do not have. He came to exchange what cannot enter into heaven with that which can enter heaven. Galatians 4:4-5 says that because sin entered God's creation, He sent His Son into the world to be born of a woman. This is the prophetic significance of Genesis 3:15. God planned His work down to the smallest detail.

> Since you have purified your souls in obeying the truth through the Spirit in sincere love of the brethren, love one another fervently with a pure heart, having been born again, not of corruptible seed but incorruptible, through the word of God which lives and abides forever.
> **1 Peter 1:22-23**

Not long after His birth in a stable, Satan's plan entered into Herod's heart to kill the baby Jesus. Satan knew that if this life ever grew up to fulfill its destiny, he would be defeated. He knew that, unless Jesus' life was destroyed, He would take away his power and destroy him. Christ the Son had been born. This life in Jesus was a life that knew no sin. It was the life of the Father in the Son. It was a life to be humanized in the body of Jesus to meet temptations as you and I meet temptations – and yet never sin. The only perfect human life, so He could be our only perfect sacrifice for sin. Jesus knew He came into the world for a purpose: not only to destroy the works of the devil, but to live a life tested in every point as we are tested, because He was going to plant a new life into man. This seed of Christ is incorruptible. When we're born again we receive this incorruptible seed within us.

In John 1:29, John the Baptist saw Jesus coming toward him and said, "Behold the Lamb of God who takes away the sin of the world!" When Jesus stepped into the Jordan River and was baptized, He had eternal life within Him. Eternal life does not mean a life sometime in the future, but it is the quality of life without end. He had within Him a life that was of the Father and knew no limitations. As John baptized Jesus, the Holy Spirit descended upon Him as a dove. He was filled with the Spirit "without measure" as the dove settled upon Him and a new era began. When Jesus was filled with the Spirit, the Spirit of God was no longer a hovering Spirit, as in the days of old. Here was the beginning of the indwelling Holy Spirit, dwelling inside of Jesus, and soon to come dwell in us also.

Jesus did not perform His miracles by His own power or deity while in human form; the miracles were performed by the power of the Holy Spirit. Why? To give us His example, showing that the Holy Spirit would also work miracles through his human followers: the disciples, the apostles, the Early Church, and eventually, through you and me as believers in Him. Even now, by the power of the Holy Spirit, great exploits can be done by us as we believe. How is this possible? It is because of this exchanged life we're now living by faith in the Son of God. "For if when we were enemies we were reconciled to God through the death of His Son, much more, having been reconciled, we shall be saved by His life" (Romans 5:10).

How then are we saved? By His life! When He died on the cross, only His body died. The life that was in Him did not die; that life had mastered death. After Jesus was crucified, His body was taken from the cross and placed in the tomb. But the life which was in Him was released from the limitations of the body and He went down into hell to seek out Satan. While people were either mourning His death or rejoicing that He was no longer there to bother them, He was very much alive. After He said, "It is finished!" He went down into hell on the prowl. He was after something. What did Adam give to Satan? The keys to death, hell, and the grave. In other words, Adam turned over the authority of this world to Satan. Up to this point, Satan held the keys to the destiny of man. Satan and all the forces in his kingdom are a symbol of darkness. Darkness does not mean blackness. It means no hope, without faith, without remedy, without restoration. In other words, there was no solution to the circumstances that held these fallen angels.

Imagine, if you can, the Eternal Light walking into darkness. I can just hear the screams of the fallen angels and satanic forces as Jesus invaded hell. Jesus was dead, but He wasn't dead! He had been crucified and His body laid to rest, but He was alive! The spirit world is even more real than the physical world in which we live. When you begin to understand the spirit world, it will put a backbone inside of you. It will put a courage and authority inside of you that you never had before. While Jesus was on earth, Satan was determined to cause Him to sin. He dogged His footsteps day and night, tormenting Him every step of the way. He was relentless, using everything he had to ruin the divine process of redemption.

But Jesus withstood him in the wilderness, on the Mount of Temptation, in the sun and in the heat, in hunger and in fasting. He especially withstood him on the cross. Jesus hung on that cross by purpose. The very reason He had come into this world was to die on that cross. He met the enemy at every turn of the road. Then, in hell, Jesus took the keys from Satan. The first thing He took was death, eternal separation from God. He also took the power of sickness to destroy the physical body. That is why there is healing in the atonement. And He took from Satan the curse which you and I had been placed under. Then He rose from the dead, triumphant!

Yes, there is warfare when Jesus builds His Church. As we build with Him, we do it with His victory. When we are born again, He gives us the keys of the Kingdom that He took back from the devil. Satan no longer possesses these keys. We do, because Jesus took back what the devil had stolen from Adam! The keys function through relationship. As we walk in relationship with God through Jesus in our redeemed life, Satan is rendered ineffective. We have power! This is the place of dominion that God wants every believer to find. The Kingdom of God is built on relationships and everything within it moves by faith, which is obedience.

> "And I will give you the keys of the kingdom of heaven, and whatever you bind on earth will be bound in heaven, and whatever you loose on earth will be loosed in heaven."
> **Matthew 16:19**

With His life, Jesus purchased our redemption, bringing us back into right relationship with the Father – the same relationship Adam had before he sinned in the garden. This new nature that He puts within us is exchanged for our old sin nature when we are born again.

In Him we live and move and have our being (Acts 17:28). We're the same person but not the same. Now we are heirs of God and joint heirs with Christ!

> For you did not receive the spirit of bondage again to fear, but you received the Spirit of adoption by whom we cry out, "Abba, Father." The Spirit Himself bears witness with our spirit that we are children of God, and if children, then heirs – heirs of God and joint heirs with Christ, if indeed we suffer with Him, that we may also be glorified together.
> **Romans 8:15–17**

A conversion experience is necessary to receive this new life. We're kept under the law until faith comes (Galatians 3:24). Faith cannot come unless it comes through Jesus Christ by the work of grace and by the Holy Spirit of God. We're saved by grace through faith (Ephesians 2:8) and when this miracle takes place, the incorruptible seed is planted into our spirit, and a whole new nature takes root: We are no longer under the old law. We're under the new law of the Spirit of life in Christ Jesus who has made us free from the law of sin and death (Romans 8:2). This is what happens when we are born again.

Do you realize what you possess as a child of God, and how privileged you really are? Quit looking at the negative! Don't look at your problems; they're not permanent! When this message presses deep enough into your spirit, your whole approach to life will be positive. God is at work in our lives to get us to the point where our entire lifestyle is one of crying out, Abba, Father! It is a life of joy, of victory and of power! Jesus is the unlimited Christ!

In our new exchanged life, we are brought back into relationship with the Father through Christ, and the work He is about to do today within the spirit of man is greater than anything He has done since the beginning of time! We're moving into the final hours of the Dispensation of Grace, the Church Age; the Holy Spirit Age. In these days, we live life by moving in the gifts of the Holy Spirit, using the keys of the Kingdom of God as we labor with Christ and He builds His Church through us! This is what makes a Walking Revival! There is no limit! The world is so dry, it's ready to catch fire!

THE GOSPEL

What does the Gospel mean? What is the essence of the Gospel? Why is the Gospel so important? These are very important questions. They are worthy of taking a few moments to clarify. Gospel means Good News. But not just any good news. When it comes to the Bible and Christianity, we're talking about the Gospel of Jesus Christ. Literally the Good News of Jesus Christ. What is the Good News? What is this Gospel? In Romans 1:16, the Apostle Paul answers it this way: "It is the power of God unto salvation to every one that believeth."

How easy it is to forget that. The Good News is that Jesus Christ came into this world for a specific reason: to die on the cross; to shed His blood – the Sinless for the guilty – in order to redeem man back into a right relationship with God. So, the Gospel has everything to do with the Kingdom of God. The Gospel has everything to do with relationships, vertical and horizontal. Love God; Love People. God created Adam for relationship. When Adam sinned, that relationship was broken. Sin separates. Jesus died to bring us back into the relationship Adam once had with God. This is the very essence of what Christianity is all about. Being born again. Reviving man's relationship with God through a supernatural spiritual birthing by the Spirit of God. Being "born from above." It is this experience that causes a sinner to come into a right relationship with God the Father.

> He indeed was foreordained before the foundation of the world, but was manifest in these last times for you who through Him believe in God, who raised Him from the dead and gave Him glory, so that your faith and hope are in God.
> **1 Peter 1:20-21**
>
> And so it is written, "The first man Adam became a living being." The last Adam became a life-giving spirit.
> **1 Corinthians 15:45**

Jesus came into the world without a sin nature. He is the Last Adam! The first Adam, in his disobedience, brought sin and death into the world. Christ, the second or Last Adam, undoes the work of the first. His obedience to the point of death brings life and righteousness.

> However, the spiritual is not first, but the natural, and afterward the spiritual. The first man was of the earth, made of dust; the second Man is the Lord from heaven. As was the man of dust, so also are those who are made of dust; and as is the heavenly Man, so also are those who are heavenly. And as we have borne the image of the man of dust, we shall also bear the image of the heavenly Man.
> **1 Corinthians 15:46-49**
>
> Therefore if any man be in Christ, he is a new creature: old things are passed away; behold, all things are become new.
> **2 Corinthians 5:17**
>
> I have been crucified with Christ; it is no longer I who live, but Christ lives in me; and the life which I now live in the flesh I live by faith in the Son of God, who loved me and gave Himself for me.
> **Galatians 2:20**

Being born again is being born by the power of God putting His divine nature into us!

> Whereby are given unto us exceeding great and precious promises: that by these ye might be partakers of the divine nature, having escaped the corruption that is in the world through lust.
> **2 Peter 1:4**

It is God's power that gives us life, both abundant and eternal! God gave of Himself for us so that we could really live a life of abundance!

> "The thief does not come except to steal, and to kill, and to destroy. I have come that they may have life, and that they may have it more abundantly."
> **John 10:10**

Only Christ Himself, this glorious treasure, can enter our lives and change us! This is the glorious treasure of Christ living within the believer – by the power of God's Holy Spirit. Living Christ daily! We're now living His life by faith. We're living for Him, not ourselves.

FOLLOW-UP

When a person initially gives their life to Jesus they're known as babes in Christ. Whatever they think they know about God and about Jesus is usually wrong. What they think they know may be mixed with so much other stuff that they are confused about what the Christian life really is. They don't know how to serve God. Most do not know how to read the Bible and they really don't know how to have victory in their lives.

Yes, I said *victory*. After being saved for a short while, I began to have a whole new set of words in my vocabulary. *Victory* was one of those words. *Having the victory* meant that I was winning one of the many battles that a Christian will face in life.

Since I was the first one saved in a newly planted church, it was my pastor, Harold Warner, who followed up on me. Almost every day, he would come by and catch me at home or just as I got off work, and spend time winning me to himself and to the church. He would talk about the things of God with me and try to answer any questions I had about being a Christian. He would encourage me to be in church the next service so I could grow in God. Basically, he helped me understand my new relationship with Jesus and became my new best friend. He was my example of what a Christian was. My relationship with God and with others was being forged in those earliest of days as a born-again believer.

The idea behind follow-up is to make contact within 24 hours after people pray to accept Jesus and begin to befriend them so the devil doesn't snatch the seed of God's Word out of their hearts before it had time to take root. Soon I became involved in follow-up, too. I was working as a cook back then, so I chose to become a breakfast cook in order to have all the time I needed to grow in God and to be in church. Opening at 4:30 a.m., I would finish my eight hours by 1:30 p.m., get home and shower, and begin to pray. Around that time, my pastor would call and give me names, addresses, and phone numbers for those who were recently saved.

In the first three years of the church, I did almost all the follow-up. The last two years before we went out to pastor, we averaged 500 new converts a year and I was serving round the clock. Not only did my pastor call to give me a list of names and info, but he would also call back within a few hours to get a report on each person. He never allowed me to be slack concerning this. I was accountable.

One young couple came into a Saturday night concert scene and gave their lives to Jesus. They came back for Sunday morning service, but not for Sunday night. On Monday evening I went to their house to follow up on them. As I reached out to them and got them talking about the things of God, the young man lit up a cigarette. He was purposely blowing smoke right into my face. I ignored the smoke and kept speaking. He told me later that he came back to church because I didn't get in his face for doing that. We became friends and 47 years later we're still friends, and we're still in the same church together. Relationships.

While pastoring in Canada during the mid-1980s, we would involve our church in street evangelism with music, drama, and preaching in downtown Vancouver. One Saturday night, a man in our congregation introduced me to a pastor he had met while witnessing. He was the pastor of a church in Hamilton, Ontario, on the other side of Canada, and supervised a sales team for a major dental company across the nation. I struck up a conversation with him and simply became his friend. He came to Vancouver about twice a month, and we always got together when he came and spoke frequently on the phone. He introduced me to a pastor friend of his from Barrie, Ontario, and through phone calls I became his friend, as well. The Spirit of God was moving mightily through me during that time in Canada, and just through friendships alone, things stirred afresh in the lives and ministries of these pastors. In 1987, I went out to the Toronto area to minister and preached in both of their churches. God moved powerfully in those meetings, solidifying our friendships even more. In February, 1989, I moved back to Tucson, Arizona to work as an evangelist from the church where I first became a Christian. Shortly after that, the pastor from Hamilton, Ontario joined me there as an evangelist. He had already given up his church in Hamilton and was stirred to work as an evangelist. Shortly after that, the pastor from Barrie, Ontario also gave up his church to work as an evangelist. All three of us began preaching throughout the world. Over thirty years have gone by since I met these two ministers and we're still very close friends to this day. They're as good a friend as you could ever ask for. Relationships.

After serving God for several years, I began realizing the depth of these relationships. There is nothing else like them. I have the best friends a person could ever hope for, let alone have. As I've watched my friends' children grow up (many from birth), get married, and have children of their own, I extend to them the same friendship. I don't violate my friends; I cherish every one of them. If there's one thing I've learned through the years, it's that the premise for being a Walking Revival is this: Love God; Love People. Relationships. This is the Kingdom of God in the earth.

THIS IS REAL REVIVAL!

What are we praying for when we pray for revival? A series of meetings? A movement? Webster's Dictionary defines revival as "an act or instance of reviving." Reviving. That means bringing back to life. Real revival is bringing us back into the relationship with God that Adam once had. It means sinners coming into a real relationship with the living God, bringing them back to life. It's what Jesus died for! It's what breaks the power of sin in our lives. Bringing Christ to others in the power of the Holy Spirit is what makes us a Walking Revival. Allowing God to work through us to build His Church. He gives us purpose in life. Something to live for.

Revival begins the moment you are born again. Are you lost? You need to be revived! Backslidden? You need to be revived! Lost your first love, Jesus? You need to be revived!

When you are revived, you come into a right relationship with your Father in heaven! When the disciples asked Jesus to teach them to pray He began with the words, Our Father. Jesus aligned Himself with us in relationship to the Father. As 100% man, He had the same relationship and dominion with God that Adam first had when God created him. Because of that relationship, He walked on earth in power, accessing all that God the Father had to offer.

That relationship was broken when Christ, our sacrifice – the One who knew no sin – became sin for us on the cross (2 Corinthians 5:21). Just before He died He cried out in Matthew 27:46, "My God, My God! Why hast thou forsaken Me?" Jesus died to bring us back into that same relationship that Adam once had: A place of dominion; a place of abundant life!

God the Father so loved His rebellious children that He went to infinite lengths to redeem them! He gave Himself in His own unique Son, Jesus the Christ, who became a living creation in body, mind, and spirit; suffering the torments of hell on the cross at Calvary. Because we are of such immense value, the ultimate price was paid by God himself in Christ, in order that "whoever believes in him should not perish but have eternal life" (John 3:16). Hallelujah!

I have to say this once again. The entire Kingdom of God is relationships. Relationship with God (vertical) and relationship with one another (horizontal). And love is the foundation of all relationships. Love God; Love People. Relationships. It is through this glorious relationship with God that He makes you into a Walking Revival.

CHAPTER THREE

TRANSFORMATION

But He needed to go through Samaria.
John 4:4

MY FIRST NIGHT IN CHURCH

The night I gave my life to Jesus Christ was very powerful. I was converted. Transformed. Changed from the inside out. I had truly been "born again." It was February 13, 1974 and that was the very first time in my life that I realized how real God is. Little did I know what He had done in my life in that moment.

January, 1974. Naomi, a woman twice my age, was hired where I worked and immediately began witnessing to me about Jesus and my need to "get saved." I went to church with her as a deal she made with me: If I would go to church with her just once, she wouldn't tell me about Jesus anymore unless I asked. I didn't plan to ask. As I listened to her talking about Jesus every day, my whole life seemed to be falling apart. The more I listened, the more things were going wrong in my life. I was totally ignorant about God and knew nothing about Christianity.

The first thing she said to me when I picked her up was, "The church I go to only speaks Spanish and I know you don't speak Spanish. So we're going to go to a little missionary church on the south side of Tucson." I asked her what a missionary church was. She told me it was the beginning of a church – not in a church building but in a smaller building. It was. On the south side of Tucson. In the worst area of town. A drug addict's haven. A shooting gallery. The church was a small and very old adobe duplex with party animals living in one unit and most of the walls knocked out in the other unit to make a very small hall. She then told me a new pastor whom she had never met was starting this church. I asked her what a pastor was. She explained the best she could. Naomi then told me they were having a revival. I asked her what a revival was. She told me it was a series of meetings with an evangelist. I asked her what an evangelist was. She told me. By this time, we had arrived at the church. Late. Service had already begun.

I followed Naomi into the church. They were all singing a fast chorus. When I say all, it was all four of them. The evangelist and his wife who stood in the front row, singing and clapping their hands; the red-faced pastor who sat in a wheelchair, leading the chorus with great enthusiasm; the young lady who sat playing an old upright piano who (I later learned) was the new pastor's wife. As we entered the building, Naomi immediately started clapping her hands and singing along with them (she knew the song by heart) as she went up the aisle and got in the row behind the evangelist. There were five of them and one of me. Being a good sinner, I immediately separated myself from them and sat two rows behind Naomi. All I could think was, *these people are nuts! They're crazy!*

I had a hard time comprehending the joy and excitement in this church service with just five people. I wasn't singing. But they sure were. They lifted their hands and sang a slow song or two. Then they all began speaking in different weird languages all at the same time. I had heard somewhere that Latin was spoken in some churches, so naturally I assumed this was Latin. It didn't bother me. It intrigued me. By this time, I felt something I had never experienced before: *The presence of God!* I will tell you more about this later.

THE OUTCAST OF OUTCASTS

In the Gospel of John chapter 4, we read that Jesus "left Judea and departed again to Galilee" (v.3). There were three routes He could have taken to Galilee. Two went around Samaria and one (the shortest) went through Samaria. John 4:4 specifically says, "But He needed to go through Samaria." As students of the Bible we must ask ourselves, why? The Jewish people of Jesus' day hated Samaritans. They were not considered pure Jews. The Samaritans claimed to have the same God as the Jews, but were called "enemies" in Ezra 4:1–6.

The Samaritans were not only seen as rebels, but also as racial half-breeds whose religion was tainted. Samaria was under Roman rule as Israel had been, and yet Jesus crossed all those racial and religious barriers to enter into Samaria. His actions alone proved He did not give in to prejudice. He saw people as people. Not one group over another. One thing to note here is the Samaritans were outcasts. They lived in the land of Palestine, but they were considered outcasts. John 4 tells us that a woman from "a city of Samaria" had come to Jacob's well to draw water. As you study out this chapter you will find this woman at the well was an outcast of outcasts.

As Jesus and His disciples reached Jacob's well, about half a mile from the city, John 4:6 says, "Jesus therefore, being wearied from His journey, sat thus by the well." The disciples had gone into the city to buy food and Jesus was now alone. Along came the woman, who had her own reasons for coming to draw water from the well at this time of day. But she wasn't alone. She was going about her daily business and had an encounter with a Jewish man who asked her for a drink of water. Jesus said to her, "Give Me a drink." (John 4:7b). He then steered the conversation into spiritual matters. She wasn't seeking to know God. It wasn't socially acceptable for a Jewish man (much less a rabbi) to speak to any woman in public – and yet she was deeply drawn into this conversation.

In studying this chapter, we realize she was the reason why Jesus needed to go through Samaria. I believe Jesus was led by the Spirit of God to minister to her and then, through her, the Spirit of God would minister to the whole city. Jesus was building His Church! It is supernatural. He was a Walking Revival.

God always works on a personal level, sending us to individual people to tell them about Jesus. Generally, the Gospel isn't spread from group to group, but from person to person. Every person you see has the same need for Jesus. Same God. Same Bible. Same need. Jesus used one conversation to change this woman's entire life. She then went into town to tell others. Jesus said that He came "to seek and to save that which was lost" (Luke 19:10). He saved the thief on the cross. He saved Saul, the chief of sinners who had been persecuting the Church. He saved the immoral Samaritan woman at Jacob's well. His desire is to save anyone who will put their trust in Him and in Him alone.

CONVICTION OF SIN

So what was it that so changed this woman on the spot that she couldn't keep it to herself, but went back into her city to tell everyone? She had a new dynamic in her life that was not there before: her encounter with Jesus. Due to her godless lifestyle, people had avoided conversation with this woman before, but now she was like a magnet. They were drawn to her, and they listened, and they were persuaded! What was different? She had been transformed, changed! She couldn't keep it to herself. She had become a Walking Revival! That fountain of living water was now flowing through her. Like an artesian well with water bubbling up from the earth, the new river of living water that Christ promised was freely flowing through her and affecting everyone around her! She was living something far beyond herself and didn't even realize it! This was supernatural! What brought about this transformation? I believe it is the same factor that makes the difference between religion and real Christianity. Let's call it conviction of sin.

One of the greatest problems in the Christian Church today is the absence of conviction of sin. God created each of us with a conscience inside which makes us aware of right and wrong. He uses our conscience to deal with us. Our words, crafted properly, can pick at the conscience of people. They may feel guilt for something they have done in the past. They might even feel remorse, which is a deep regret or guilt over a committed wrong. But this is not the conviction of sin. It's part of it. But conviction of sin goes much deeper.

Conviction of sin is the realization that our very natures are sinful. When truly convicted of sin, you realize that you sin because your very nature is wrong and perverted and polluted. Jesus tells the woman of Samaria, "Go, call your husband, and come here" (John 4:16). Then in verse 29, she tells the people in town, "Come see a Man who told me all things that I ever did. Could this be the Christ?" She realized her sin nature. For the first time, she saw herself for what she was. She understood that her trouble was not that she did wrong things, but that her heart was wrong; her desires were wrong. She was a sinner!

King David had committed terrible sins. But he was perfectly happy until God sent him Nathan the Prophet; then he saw it all. He had such a clear picture of his sin. He saw his nature! What troubled David was not the adultery and murder that he had committed, but the thought that he had even desired to do these things. He saw there was something in him that produced these desires. So he cried out in agony, "Create in me a clean heart, O God; and renew a right spirit within me" (Psalm 51:10). His conviction and repentance went beyond the realm of actions to the heart of his condition; to his sinful state that was motivating his whole life! He realized his very heart was foul and ugly and vile. He realized his whole spirit was wrong! This is true conviction of sin: when you are not as troubled about the things you do, as about what you are. You see the root of the matter: your entire hopeless, sinful condition.

Conviction of sin always creates within us the realization that we have sinned against God! The people of this world – even those who are moral or religious – can only see as far as themselves. They see they have let themselves or others down or they have done something they shouldn't have. What will people say? What will the consequences be? God does not even figure in their scenario. But the moment they are truly convicted of sin by the Holy Spirit, their whole concern is that they have sinned against God and that they have broken His holy laws.

> Have mercy upon me, O God, According to Your lovingkindness; According to the multitude of Your tender mercies, Blot out my transgressions. Wash me thoroughly from my iniquity, And cleanse me from my sin. For I acknowledge my transgressions, And my sin is always before me. Against You, You only, have I sinned, And done this evil in Your sight – That You may be found just when You speak, And blameless when You judge.
> **Psalm 51:1-4**

This is what now troubles David. He sees the enormity of his sin! He is no longer concerned about the wrong things he has done, but that he has done them against God! So have we all. We have let God down! The God who made us! The God who has been so kind! The God who has been so loving toward us! We deliberately went against His laws. We've wounded Him! We have hurt Him! We have violated what He intended us to be! Now we see our sin – not merely as a matter of wrong actions, but we see it as it is. It is lawlessness! It is arrogance! We're against God! We have rebelled against Him!

This is the response of the prodigal son after he has "come to himself." He sees he has sinned against his father, sinned against the one who showered his love upon him and did so much for him! This is what he sees as unforgivable. "I have sinned against heaven, and in thy sight, and am no more worthy to be called thy son" (Luke 15:18-19, 21). He now sees his actions in a true way. Our personal relationship with God is what is at stake; restoring it is what conviction of sin is all about!

Real conviction of sin and repentance is a feeling of true sorrow. The Apostle Paul calls it godly sorrow. "For godly sorrow produces repentance leading to salvation, not to be regretted" (2 Corinthians 7:10).

Godly sorrow is very difficult to define. It's not a mild irritation or annoyance with yourself! No. It is much deeper. You are troubled! You are grieved! Godly sorrow is deeper than a surface emotion or some temporary feeling. People who've been convicted of sin always realize that their first and most desperate need is mercy; that they need forgiveness! We're acutely aware that, more than anything else, we need the compassion of God!

In Luke 18:13, Jesus told of the Pharisee and the tax collector going up to the Temple to pray. The Pharisee is proudly praying, but the poor tax collector stands in the shadows and cannot even lift up his head. He can only beat his chest and say, "God, be merciful to me a sinner!" He is so aware of his sin that he realizes his greatest needs are for forgiveness, mercy, and compassion. Someone who is convicted of sin has a great desire to be free from sin! This is where true repentance takes place.

When revival breaks out, the first effect of the Spirit of God upon a people, a congregation, a group of churches, or a nation is invariably conviction of utter sinfulness. It always happens! It has always happened. Revival is in the Church! Not outside! It is in the person! What matters is not the number of sins we've committed, nor their character or quality! What matters alone is our relationship to God! When you come into God's presence, you realize the truth about yourself. One of the prevailing factors of the Jesus People Movement of the late '60s and early '70s was the conviction of sin. The revival was not spear-headed by any one person or group. It was the result of God's Holy Spirit moving on an entire generation of lost, self-destructive young people. God sovereignly moved and saved my generation from utter destruction.

THE NIGHT OF MY SALVATION

The night I was saved was during the Jesus People Movement. By the time the evangelist began to preach, I was very aware of the presence of God. I began feeling and sensing something that I had never experienced before. Within moments, I had a great awareness of the reality of God. As he continued preaching, this awareness kept getting stronger. I was being overwhelmed by the fact that God existed, that He was holy, and that I was in big trouble. Halfway through his preaching, I put my hands under my thighs on the chair because my hands were shaking under the conviction of sin and I felt I had to hide that because I was sure everyone was looking at me. It had nothing to do with the message. It was conviction of sin! The Holy Spirit of God was dealing with me about my sin and the lost condition of my soul! Godly sorrow was setting in. It was about to bring forth repentance.

At the end of his message, Evangelist Jack Harris (preaching his very first revival) had everyone bow their heads and close their eyes, and pleaded with us (literally, with me) to surrender to Jesus. He made a call to raise my hand if I wanted to "get saved" by giving my life to Jesus. After hesitating several times, I raised my hand slightly above my thigh, and quickly I heard, "God sees that hand!" I pulled my hand down just as quickly. I stared at the floor. Thoughts were racing through my head. When he made the plea for me to come forward, I didn't move. His voice got louder as he walked down the aisle toward me. I looked up. He was practically in front of me. "I'm talking to you!" he said. Everything inside me cried out, Run! I shot a desperate glance at the door. He was still coming. "Get up out of your chair and come to the front and pray!" he said. Slowly I got up and he coaxed me forward. He moved aside as I got to the front and Pastor Harold Warner wheeled his chair over to me. I thought, I don't want this lame man praying for me! How wicked our hearts are and we don't even know it until we come into the presence of God.

Pastor Warner asked me if I was there to give my life to Jesus. I shrugged my shoulders and said I didn't know why I was there. He then told me I was there to give my life to Jesus! He leaned forward, grabbed my arm, and pulled me down. "Get on your knees!" he said. "We're going to pray!" I told him I didn't know how to pray. He said he would lead me in a prayer and all I had to do was believe with all my heart and repeat after him. So I did.

By the time I had finished the sinner's prayer, I was weeping uncontrollably. This freaked me out, because I couldn't remember the last time I had cried for anything. I had a hard heart.

As I calmed down, Pastor Warner told me I needed to be in church now that I was a Christian. I said, "Okay. I'll go back to the Mormon church. It's the only church I've ever known."

"They're not telling the truth!" he said.

"They're not?"

"Have you ever heard a message like this in the Mormon church?" he asked.

"No."

"Because they're not telling the truth!"

"Okay," I said.

I had been born and raised a Mormon; at that moment, twenty years of Mormonism had been erased from my life. I was instantly set free from their teaching. I never did struggle with the false teachings of the Mormons' Jesus. I was totally set free! The real Jesus had just saved me! When you are genuinely converted to Christ, the Spirit of God begins leading you into all truth.

It was a very supernatural night for me. The presence of God brought conviction of sin, which caused godly sorrow that led to repentance. I was born again! Converted. Changed. Transformed. Jesus was very real to me from that moment on. My whole life had changed and I began living for God.

Pastor Warner told me to tell someone about Jesus as soon as I could, making a stand for Jesus. I came home that night to a party. My roommate met me at the front door and pushed a joint in my mouth. I shoved it aside and he immediately said, "Beau? What are you high on? You're smiling from ear to ear! You must have had some really good stuff!"

"I'm not high!" I said. "I just gave my life to Jesus Christ! I'm a Christian now! I don't need to get high any longer. I have something better!"

"Oh, Beau! No!" he said as I walked past him and into my room, closing the door behind me. I found my Bible and began to read it. Within a few minutes the party was over and everybody had left. The next day, my roommate told me I was just passing through a phase in my life. It would only last a couple of weeks. He had no idea of the profound experience I had just had with God. I was forever changed! Transformed!

The greatest sin of all is the failure to see your need for salvation. It's much worse than murder, since we all nailed Jesus to the cross for our sins. To think you can stand in the presence of God because you are who you are and what you are, or because of what you have or have not done, is the greatest of all sins! It means that you think you do not need the death of the Son of God on the cross at Calvary. Men and women who attain to the greatest heights in their Christian lives and receive the fullness of God are those who have been under the deepest depths of conviction over their sin and have realized their utter hopelessness. Jesus had an encounter with another woman in Luke chapter 7 who recognized her sin and God's love.

> "Therefore I say to you, her sins, which are many, are forgiven, for she loved much. But to whom little is forgiven, the same loves little." Then He said to her, "Your sins are forgiven."
> **Luke 7:47-48**

This woman was the type of sinner that was rejected by the religious leaders, the Pharisees. She was so convicted of her sinful life that she humbled herself, weeping as she knelt at Jesus' feet. Conviction of sin brings forth true repentance which requires humility. "But He gives more grace. Therefore He says: God resists the proud, but gives grace to the humble" (James 4:6). She was transformed, expressing great love toward God and others, because much had been forgiven. As a result, it was in her to share Christ with others. It flowed out of her. Transformation will bring a new dynamic of joy into your life and you cannot easily hide it. You don't want to.

We've looked at only one element of revival in John chapter 4. But every element you will find in any genuine move of God is found in the story of the Woman at the Well. Study any move of God anywhere in the world over the last 2,000 years and you will see that every one of them had these same elements. The Church that Jesus was building was now being built through the woman at the well. She had become a Walking Revival! She was truly born again because of conviction of her sin by the Holy Spirit which led to godly sorrow and caused genuine repentance. This same process also transformed your life and now His life is flowing through you. The degree of your godly sorrow and your surrender to God on the inside will lead to others being attracted to you by the Spirit of God. Now, God is supernaturally moving through you to be a witness of the indwelling Christ. I hope you're beginning to get the picture of what a Walking Revival is all about.

CHAPTER FOUR

SEED

"And to your Seed," who is Christ.
Galatians 3:16

THE SEED HAS A HISTORY

The concept of seed is a very important one to understand as a believer in Jesus Christ. It is a revelation. My hope and prayer is that God will open your heart and understanding to this wonderful and powerful truth.

> And the earth brought forth grass, the herb that yields seed according to its kind, and the tree that yields fruit, whose seed is in itself according to its kind. And God saw that it was good.
> **Genesis 1:12**

In the spring of every year, my mother and father would plant a garden. The whole family of ten would go to the hardware store and each of the kids picked out a package of seeds we wanted to plant. It was our choice. Naturally, the seeds produced the same kind of vegetable whose name was on the package. I would go out to the garden several times a day to look closely at what I had planted. The proof of the seed was a tender little shoot coming up from the earth. Life was in that seed. I was thrilled to see life and couldn't wait until it grew and matured so I could eat it.

Now I want to look with you at another seed, the Seed of Christ. This seed has a history. It begins in the Garden of Eden.

> "And I will put enmity Between you and the woman, And between your seed and her Seed; He shall bruise your head, And you shall bruise His heel."
>
> **Genesis 3:15**

The Seed next appears in Scripture as the Seed of Abraham (Genesis 28:14). Here we find that God limits the promise of the coming Christ to a single family in the world. The first promise shows He would be virgin born and a member of the human race. This next promise makes Him a member of the Hebrew family.

Later, the seed is shown to be the Seed of David, meaning Messiah would not only be a member of any Hebrew family, but a member of the Hebrew royal family. He tells David:

> Moreover I will appoint a place for My people Israel, and will plant them, that they may dwell in a place of their own and move no more; nor shall the sons of wickedness oppress them anymore, as previously, since the time that I commanded judges to be over My people Israel, and have caused you to rest from all your enemies. Also the LORD tells you that He will make you a house. "When your days are fulfilled and you rest with your fathers, I will set up your seed after you, who will come from your body, and I will establish his kingdom. He shall build a house for My name, and I will establish the throne of his kingdom forever. I will be his Father, and he shall be My son. If he commits iniquity, I will chasten him with the rod of men and with the blows of the sons of men. But My mercy shall not depart from him, as I took it from Saul, whom I removed from before you. And your house and your kingdom shall be established forever before you. Your throne shall be established forever." According to all these words and according to all this vision, so Nathan spoke to David.
>
> **2 Sam. 7:10–17**

The history of the Seed can be clearly traced throughout the Bible. Matthew chapter 1 shows us the genealogy of the Seed.

PAUL'S REVELATION

The apostle Paul deliberately uses the word seed in Galatians 3 to draw attention to Christ as the designated Seed of Abraham. I believe this was a foundational revelation given to Paul. One that he lived and taught daily.

> Now to Abraham and his Seed were the promises made. He does not say, "And to seeds," as of many, but as of one, "And to your Seed," who is Christ.
> **Galatians 3:16**

Paul tells the church at Galatia that the true Seed is Christ. It was Jesus to whom the promise pointed. All of the other promises centered in Him. To share in the promises of God, you must belong to Christ.

> And if you are Christ's, then you are Abraham's seed, and heirs according to the promise.
> **Galatians 3:29**

The Judaizers had been "bewitching" the Galatian believers. The word bewitched means: "to be placed under an evil spell; to cast a spell upon; to mislead; to deceive." Gentile Christians had been saved by grace. But the Judaizers were telling them they needed the addition of the Mosaic Law and circumcision to truly be God's people. This was warfare in the building of His Church.

Paul battles it out with the Judaizers. They taught salvation as a combination of faith and works (which, Scripture says, results in a curse). To avoid this spiritual curse, you must refuse to depend on the Law for salvation (outward). Paul wanted to make it absolutely clear that we are justified only by our faith (inward); not by merit, nor by good works or moral excellence (outward).

All the promises God made to Abraham are fulfilled by Jesus the Christ and given to us. His sacrifice was for everyone of us because Paul writes: "that the blessing of Abraham might come upon the Gentiles in Christ Jesus, that we might receive the promise of the Spirit through faith" (Galatians 3:14).

Abraham did not make a promise to God. God made a promise to Abraham. Promises depend 100% on God. Not on what we do. God never breaks His promises.

> I will make you a great nation; I will bless you And make your name great; And you shall be a blessing.
> **Genesis 12:2**
>
> Not a word failed of any good thing which the LORD had spoken to the house of Israel. All came to pass.
> **Joshua 21:45**

The fulfillment of God's promise to Abraham didn't reside in the Jewish people or in the Law, but in Christ. In other words, the law and the promise cannot be mixed or combined to secure our salvation. Our inheritance (salvation) doesn't depend on the Law (our performance) but on grace (God's promise).

> For if the inheritance comes by the law, it no longer comes by promise; but God gave it to Abraham by a promise.
> **Galatians 3:18**

God wants us to live for Him in love and faith, not under the Law and fear. He wants to have a relationship with us in the same context as the promise He gave to Abraham, not in the context in which He gave the Law. The Law reveals our need of a Savior, and the promise reveals the fulfillment of that need. The Law cannot, and was never intended to, give life. The Law always makes demands, but has nothing to give.

The Law is us working in our own power, according to our own rules, to earn God's favor. That's not the Gospel. We are saved through faith alone. God's pleasure in us is based on Christ's performance for us and not our own. As we trust in Christ, we are accepted by God and we become alive to Him.

In Galatians 3, Paul covers 2,000 years of Old Testament history from Abraham through Moses to Christ. The climax of all history – not only biblical history, but all history – centers on Christ. The promise given to Abraham and the law given to Moses were both given to point us to Christ. Jesus fulfills the law of Moses, and Jesus completes the promise to Abraham. That's why salvation comes only through Christ.

THE POWER OF THE SEED

Seed produces life. Life comes from God. Take a seed, any seed. Plant it. All is darkness around it. This seed will draw from that darkness everything it needs to produce life and growth. The proof that something is planted is a tender little shoot coming up from the earth. When we're born again, the life of Christ is planted within. That life is surrounded by darkness. Our darkness. The darkness of this world. The darkness of our hearts. As His life grows within by faith, here will be revival and we will bear fruit, and that fruit will remain.

> And He said, "The kingdom of God is as if a man should scatter seed on the ground, and should sleep by night and rise by day, and the seed should sprout and grow, he himself does not know how. For the earth yields crops by itself: first the blade, then the head, after that the full grain in the head. But when the grain ripens, immediately he puts in the sickle, because the harvest has come."
>
> **Mark 4:26-29**

This seed of the old life we were born with came through Adam. Now Jesus came to bring a new life by planting the seed of a new nature and that's why Paul could write, "Till the seed should come to whom the promise was made" (Galatians 3:19). We are born again by the incorruptible seed. "Being born again, not of corruptible seed, but of incorruptible, by the word of God, which liveth and abideth forever" (1 Peter 1:23). Look with me at the parable of the seed and the soil.

> "Now the parable is this: The seed is the word of God. Those by the wayside are the ones who hear; then the devil comes and takes away the word out of their hearts, lest they should believe and be saved. But the ones on the rock are those who, when they hear, receive the word with joy; and these have no root, who believe for a while and in time of temptation fall away. Now the ones that fell among thorns are those who, when they have heard, go out and are choked with cares, riches, and pleasures of life, and bring no fruit to maturity. But the ones that fell on the good ground are those who, having heard the word with a noble and good heart, keep it and bear fruit with patience."
> **Luke 8:11–15**

The seed is perfect. The seed is Christ. The problem is the soil, or literally a person's heart, where the seed is received. When the seed is put into the ground and buried, the darkness surrounding that seed causes it to be broken. It is through that brokenness life begins to grow. It usually takes crisis, sorrow, heartache, and pressure to break the human heart within us. Only through this process of brokenness can the seed begin to grow. Our hearts are already full of darkness, wickedness, and every evil thing. Look at these Scriptures:

> Then the LORD saw that the wickedness of man was great in the earth, and that every intent of the thoughts of his heart was

only evil continually. And the LORD was sorry that He had made man on the earth, and He was grieved in His heart.
Genesis 6:5–6

And the LORD smelled a soothing aroma. Then the LORD said in His heart, "I will never again curse the ground for man's sake, although the imagination of man's heart is evil from his youth; nor will I again destroy every living thing as I have done. "While the earth remains, seedtime and harvest, cold and heat, winter and summer, and day and night shall not cease."
Genesis 8:21–22

"The heart is deceitful above all things, and desperately wicked; who can know it? I, the LORD, search the heart, I test the mind, even to give every man according to his ways, according to the fruit of his doings."
Jeremiah 17:9–10

"Brood of vipers! How can you, being evil, speak good things? For out of the abundance of the heart the mouth speaks."
Matthew 12:34

This is the heart of your old nature. Through conviction of sin, your hard heart is being broken and this precious seed of Christ is planted. Out of that darkness and brokenness, life begins to grow. What kind of soil is your heart? Is it the soil by the wayside? Is your heart like being on the rock which has no root in itself? Or is it like being among the thorns where life is being choked out? Hopefully, your heart is good ground. Then God will plow the soil to receive the seed. Circumstances coming into your life break up the fallow ground of your heart. The seed is planted and watered with tears and prayer. This is where it takes root and grows out of the darkness of your heart.

All of us come from different backgrounds and God deals with us differently. He will deal with us patiently and in answer to prayer. So don't be angry with God if something happens that you don't understand. Our natural state coming into this world is spiritual death.

We're not dead biologically, but we are dead to God. You can only have the tremendous life Jesus promised through a new birth, by the planting of the incorruptible seed into your spirit. Jesus had to perfect the seed so that it wouldn't just cleanse us, but bring us a new life. A new nature has to be planted. This was the purpose of Calvary and the reason Jesus came. This is why there was warfare and He was tested. He went into hell and took back the keys. Until then, Satan had control of physical death. But the Seed was being made complete. Jesus had to rise from the dead before He could be accepted by the Father and sit at His right hand. There He was accepted and restored to the glory He had laid aside in order to come to earth. Once He was accepted by the Father, His life could be planted into your spirit and mine through the Holy Spirit. This is a miracle. The life that He lived can now be planted into our spirits. Now that we have been cleansed of our sins, we have a new nature through the Word, the incorruptible Seed. This Word is powerful. The Holy Spirit can take the Seed of the Living Word, Jesus, plant it into our spirits which before were dead to God, and begin feeding it until there is a new man.

This life within you is the very treasure of the Father. It is the life of His Son. It's the Seed called the Word of God, Jesus. That Seed is absolutely perfect. Everything heaven has for man is in that Seed. God prepared it through the life Jesus lived. That's why we don't have to say, "Lord, I want an overcoming life." You already have it! It's already in you, it just hasn't been worked out yet. He has to get past our old nature.

This life of Christ has already mastered the enemy, been glorified by the Father and was given into the hands of the Holy Spirit to sow the Seed of the Gospel into the hearts of men and women all over the world. That is why we can preach the Gospel.

The Seed, the Word of God, is sown into four different kinds of soil. We're all made different. There are some that make it and some that don't. The world is out to harden you so you will not receive the Seed. Satan wants you filled with doubt, filled with animosity, filled with hate, filled with everything that comes of his seed. What is this world built on? It's built upon the fallen nature of man, the seed of the fallen Adam. It's built upon the nature of death. This world is in the grip of death itself. Anything to do with death has decay and so every natural condition is going to get worse. Many things will happen because the world won't let this Gospel be sown into hearts willingly.

But this world does not know the power of the resurrected Christ. There is one thing about this Gospel: it can never be stopped because there is no death in it. Paul writes:

> For I am not ashamed of the gospel of Christ, for it is the power of God to salvation for everyone who believes, for the Jew first and also for the Greek. For in it the righteousness of God is revealed from faith to faith; as it is written, "The just shall live by faith."
> **Romans 1:16-17**
>
> Who has saved us and called us with a holy calling, not according to our works, but according to His own purpose and grace which was given to us in Christ Jesus before time began, but has now been revealed by the appearing of our Savior Jesus Christ, who has abolished death and brought life and immortality to light through the gospel,
> **2 Timothy 1:9-10**

Jesus abolished death and brought life and immortality to light through the Gospel. Spiritual death and physical death have both been abolished. And what did Jesus bring? Life! The opposite of death.

> And this is the testimony: that God has given us eternal life, and this life is in His Son. He who has the Son has life; he who does not have the Son of God does not have life.
> **John 5:11–12**

The Gospel and the entire purpose of God in bringing man to heaven have to do with only one thing: the planting of the resurrection life of Jesus within us. This is the essence of the Gospel in a nutshell. As we walk in this life of Christ within us, we become a Walking Revival. We become a threat to everything the devil stands for. God now moves through us to reach others with this glorious Gospel.

FAITH AT WORK

The entire Kingdom of God is relationships. Vertical and horizontal. By faith we're brought into right relationship with God the Father through Christ (vertical), which in turn brings us into right relationship with one another (horizontal). It's all about relationship. But everything within the Kingdom of God moves by faith. The Seed of Christ is the foundation of our faith! We're to look unto Jesus, the author and finisher of our faith (Hebrews 12:2).

When Abraham was 100 years old and Sarah was 90, their son Isaac, in whom the Seed was to be called, was born contrary to nature, as a miracle. Abraham didn't come to Sarah one day, grab her hand and say, "Hurry up, Sarah! Come on! I'm feeling faith right now!" – and then along came Isaac. No, Isaac was a result of Abraham's faith in God's promise. The Seed at work. David, coming out against Goliath, had this same Seed faith flowing through him. The disciples failed to cast demons out of a boy, but this same Seed faith moved through Jesus as He cast the demons out. Later, when Peter and John went through the Gate called Beautiful (Acts 3), it was this same Seed faith which came by promise, causing Peter to minister healing to the crippled man. Christ builds His church through the Seed faith which comes through the promises of God and is activated through our obedience to His Holy Spirit's prompting. This is where the abundant life Christ offers is lived out in the everyday.

> And fixing his eyes on him, with John, Peter said, "Look at us." So he gave them his attention, expecting to receive something from them. Then Peter said, "Silver and gold I do not have, but what I do have I give you: In the name of Jesus Christ of Nazareth, rise up and walk." And he took him by the right hand and lifted him up, and immediately his feet and ankle bones received strength. So he, leaping up, stood and walked and entered the temple with them – walking, leaping, and praising God. And all the people saw him walking and praising God. Then they knew that it was he who sat begging alms at the Beautiful Gate of the temple; and they were filled with wonder and amazement at what had happened to him.
> **Acts 3:4–10**

Jesus paid the ultimate price on Calvary's cross as Seed faith played out through His obedience. We are saved by grace alone through faith alone in Christ alone! Christ is the Seed of Abraham!

> For by grace you have been saved through faith, and that not of yourselves; it is the gift of God, not of works, lest anyone should boast.
> **Ephesians 2:8–9**

Grace is God's mercy coming to you and planting into your heart what you didn't have – faith. Faith can be measured. You weren't born with faith, but you were born with the ability to believe. Believing is not faith. Believing can move us to the place where grace comes into action and faith can be planted. God is the author of faith and through the life of Jesus, His life was planted in you. That's why you have become a new creation with a new nature.

That new nature is the miracle. The life you have in Christ Jesus met the devil, defeated him and then gave us the victory. You have a Seed that has everything inside it that heaven has, and it will defeat every work of the enemy that is, that has been, or that can ever be in your life. You have the victory already within you; it just needs working out. You're the privileged vehicle through which God manifests Jesus Christ by the Holy Spirit within your life. May God make this real to our hearts.

The devil's business is to stop the stream that feeds your life. The life that is in you is not sufficient in itself. It must be constantly supplied by the Holy Spirit, so that Christ may be fully formed in you. The life within us must increase, or else it will decrease. "You are of God, little children, and have overcome them, because He who is in you is greater than he who is in the world" (1 John 4:4). As His life increases in you, so does the victory!

In this Christian life we begin in the Spirit, but then we may try to perfect it in the flesh. That's why our spiritual man has to be fed on spiritual things. The spirit has been put back on the throne and into the relationship under the Kingship it deserves. The devil comes and tries to take that life away. How? By the lack of prayer, God's Word, and fellowship with the Body of Christ; and by disobedience to the truth. There are all kinds of things in the world wanting to invade you and choke His life out of you. God means what He says about playing with truth. Disobedience puts you on the defensive. You'll be like Adam when you disobey God: you'll be hiding and God will have to come seeking you. You become a fugitive. You become separated from Him. The entire Kingdom of God moves by faith. Every Walking Revival moves by faith. Salvation and the indwelling life of Christ all come by faith.

"IN CHRIST"

The moment we give our lives to Jesus and we are born again, we are in Christ. The phrase "in Christ" is found more than eighty times in Paul's epistles. The phrase "in Him" occurs about 30 times. This means something. Study this out. Learn from it. When we receive Christ by faith, we are spiritually baptized into Christ and we put on Christ (Galatians 3:27). It's not our life we're living but His life. Spiritually speaking, this means that God never sees us unless we are in Christ.

"If you are Christ's, then you are Abraham's offspring, and heirs according to promise" (Galatians 3:29). Christ is the true offspring, the Seed of Abraham. As we place our faith in Him, the Holy Spirit makes us one in Christ. Therefore, we become the true offspring of Abraham. We now live the life of Christ daily by faith!

> I have been crucified with Christ; it is no longer I who live, but Christ lives in me; and the life which I now live in the flesh I live by faith in the Son of God, who loved me and gave Himself for me. I do not set aside the grace of God; for if righteousness comes through the law, then Christ died in vain.
> **Galatians 2:20–21**

I live His life through me by faith. I'm still me, but I'm not what I used to be. Christ now lives in me. This is a life of victory! It is an abundant life!

> For by one Spirit we were all baptized into one body – whether Jews or Greeks, whether slaves or free – and have all been made to drink into one Spirit.
> **1 Corinthians 12:13**

A LIFE OF VICTORY

Many professing Christians today make promises to God which they can never keep. This happens because they lack knowledge of God's grace through faith. They hear a sermon, go to the altar, and make all kinds of promises to God. They live by hope rather than living by faith. Hope is not faith. They are constantly living from one struggle to another, never able to really break free and live the abundant life that Christ died to give them. Paul wrote in 2 Corinthians 5:17, "Therefore, if anyone is in Christ, he is a new creation; old things have passed away; behold, all things have become new." A lot of preaching today fails to teach the reality of this scripture in the life of a believer.

Many churches today are filled with people who are not walking in this great revelation. Old things are passed away! All things have become new! We're to walk in this truth daily! We're called to live a victorious life! That life is found only in Christ! Paul lived his Christian life with this powerful revelation as to who we are in Christ.

When my wife and I went out in February 1979 to pioneer a church in Silver City, New Mexico, we had no idea what God was going to do. On the third Sunday after we opened, an older woman named Caroline came in. We later learned that she had become a Christian just before moving back to Silver recently to take care of her aging parents, and so she was looking for a church. Her experience at the church she attended the week before ours was not fun. New to this church and new to Christ, Caroline sat down before the service began and was promptly approached by a rude woman who told her she was sitting in "her" seat. She moved to another seat, but she never went back to that church.

After my sermon, I made an appeal for anyone needing prayer for just about anything. You do that when you're starting a church and have only a few people. Caroline came forward for prayer to break the cigarette habit she had for many years. As I lay my hand on her head, she immediately fell backward, slain by the power of God. I never had this happen before so I was caught off guard and, quickly grabbing her arm, I helped her to the floor. She was immediately filled with the Spirit of God and began speaking in tongues – something I hadn't even preached on. When she got up, she was full of the Holy Spirit and never smoked another cigarette. About a year after she came that first time, she brought her son Allen to church.

For three years, Allen had been living in the mountain wilderness outside of Silver City where he grew marijuana and had two mules and a dog named Jeep (4-Paw-Drive). He was very antisocial and Caroline rarely ever saw him. He came to Silver to get supplies one Tuesday and she convinced him to listen to a taped sermon by Evangelist Larry Reed. Larry Reed was a Walking Revival. Allen was stirred by the message. Caroline invited him to come to our Wednesday night service before heading back to the wilderness for the next three months.

As I finished preaching that night, I made an appeal for those who needed Jesus as their Savior. I had everyone bow their heads and close their eyes and I said, "If that's you tonight, just lift your hand and say, 'that's me.'" Allen immediately raised his hand and shouted out a few times, "That's me! That's me!" as he shook under the conviction of the Spirit of God. In all the years that I've served God, I've never had anyone else speak that out loud before or since. We had been going through a bit of a dry spell during which no one had been saved for a few months. When he shouted that out, the church began to pray a little louder with great excitement.

As Caroline drove Allen home after the service, he asked her to pull into a drive-thru liquor store so he could buy some beer to celebrate his new-found faith in Jesus. She told him he didn't need to do that now, because Christians don't drink. He simply said, "Oh. Okay." And that was that. The seed of Christ had been planted. He had been transformed. The promises of God were now being lived out by Allen.

Years later, Allen and his wife, Rose, moved to Albuquerque, New Mexico to pioneer a church which is doing well to this day. After pastoring there for a few years, they ended up going to Kingston, Jamaica and pastoring there for several years. Allen and Rose live victorious Christian lives to this day. Caroline was faithful to church and greatly loved by everyone in the Silver City congregation right up until her home-going to heaven at 97 years of age. What a great blessing she was to everyone.

GREAT POSSIBILITIES

The moment we are saved, we are changed! The Seed is planted! Are we perfect? No. Do we understand it? No.

> Therefore be patient, brethren, until the coming of the Lord. See how the farmer waits for the precious fruit of the earth, waiting patiently for it until it receives the early and latter rain.
> **James 5:7**

Out of the darkness comes forth life! His life. We are given power to walk in life. Walk in this! We are Christians because of what He has done, not because of what we do. Jesus said, "It is finished!" Paul writes:

> I say then: Walk in the Spirit, and you shall not fulfill the lust of the flesh. For the flesh lusts against the Spirit, and the Spirit against the flesh; and these are contrary to one another, so that you do not do the things that you wish. But if you are led by the Spirit, you are not under the law.
> **Galatians 5:16–18**

Look at these scriptures that reveal who we are in Christ:

> And if children, then heirs – heirs of God and joint heirs with Christ, if indeed we suffer with Him, that we may also be glorified together.
> **Romans 8:17**

> Gentiles are fellow heirs and fellow members of the body, and fellow partakers of the promise in Christ Jesus through the gospel.
> **Ephesians 3:6**

> But when the kindness and the love of God our Savior toward man appeared, not by works of righteousness which we have done, but according to His mercy He saved us, through the washing of regeneration and renewing of the Holy Spirit, whom He poured out on us abundantly through Jesus Christ our Savior, that having been justified by His grace we should become heirs according to the hope of eternal life.
> **Titus 3:4-7**

> Listen, my beloved brethren: Has God not chosen the poor of this world to be rich in faith and heirs of the kingdom which He promised to those who love Him?
> **James 2:5**

> For not even those who are circumcised keep the law, but they desire to have you circumcised that they may boast in your flesh. But God forbid that I should boast except in the cross of our Lord Jesus Christ, by whom the world has been crucified to me, and I to the world. For in Christ Jesus neither circumcision nor uncircumcision avails anything, but a new creation.
> **Galatians 6:13–15**

BREAKTHROUGH

Do you want real breakthrough? Breakthrough is not a feeling, or the feeling that "I finally got help." Real breakthrough is Christ breaking through in our lives like a tender little shoot, for all the world to see! He will build His Church through us! Christ is the magnet within that draws people to God! We become a Walking Revival!

> "Most assuredly, I say to you, unless a grain of wheat falls into the ground and dies, it remains alone; but if it dies, it produces much grain."
> **John 12:24**

CHAPTER FIVE

FAITH

There remains therefore a rest for the people of God.
Hebrews 4:9

THE "REST" IN FAITH

In order to be a Walking Revival you must walk in faith. I'm not talking about some kind of hype. I'm talking real faith. God, by His grace, has given everyone of us a measure of faith. From the moment you are born again, you begin walking in this faith. It's not something you have to "work up." Either you have it or you don't.

> For I say, through the grace given to me, to everyone who is among you, not to think of himself more highly than he ought to think, but to think soberly, as God has dealt to each one a measure of faith.
> **Romans 12:3**

Real faith is based in God's Word. As we grow in God we can also grow in faith. Do you want more faith? Go to God's Word. "So then faith comes by hearing, and hearing by the word of God" (Romans 10:17). When you walk in a genuine God-given faith, you will be at rest. There is no fighting within you, just a settled peace with God. Faith has a natural flow to it.

The "rest" found in Hebrews 4 stands out as you read its first eleven verses. In the English translation, the word rest appears here nine times. This is significant. We can learn something here. The scripture reveals the nature of the rest that God offers: it is the same rest in which He rested on the seventh day after creating the world. Faith is the key. We enter this rest only after ceasing from our own works – from facing the struggles of life on our own (v. 10).

Israel had wandered in the wilderness for forty years – a whole generation – because divine wrath had come against their unbelief. That wrath confirms that faith was necessary for entering into the Land of Promise. If we operate under unbelief, we live in a constant struggle. No peace. No faith. No rest. Only turmoil. Everything in the Kingdom of God moves by faith. God's rest comes as we live by faith; laying claim to God's promises and inheriting them.

The chief burden of the entire epistle to the Hebrews is to encourage believers to go on in the Christian life of faith. To persevere. These eleven verses tell us about the children of Israel in the wilderness. They had sent twelve spies into the Land of Promise and ten came back bringing an "evil report of unbelief" (Hebrews 3:18-19). Two brought back a report of victory: Joshua and Caleb rested in the promises of God (Seed of Abraham) no matter what kind of enemy they had seen in the Land of Promise.

> But Joshua the son of Nun and Caleb the son of Jephunneh, who were among those who had spied out the land, tore their clothes; and they spoke to all the congregation of the children of Israel, saying: "The land we passed through to spy out is an exceedingly good land. If the LORD delights in us, then He will bring us into this land and give it to us, 'a land which flows with milk and honey.' Only do not rebel against the LORD, nor fear the people of the land, for they are our bread; their protection has departed from them, and the LORD is with us. Do not fear them." And all the congregation said to stone them with stones.
> **Numbers 14:6–10**

The people sided with ten unbelievers and had murder in their hearts toward those who believed. The unbelief in their hearts caused them to hate anyone who did not think as they thought. No faith, no joy, and no peace. Especially, no rest. Unbelief fails to enter into God's rest. It fails to believe the promises of God! The Hebrews at Kadesh-Barnea failed in identifying with the faith of Joshua and Caleb to believe the promises of God. So, the good report that these faithful men brought back did not help the people.

> For we who have believed do enter that rest, as He has said: "So I swore in My wrath, 'They shall not enter My rest,' "although the works were finished from the foundation of the world.
> **Hebrews 4:3**

Those who believe enter into God's rest. Faith is His ordained way of appropriating the promises which come through the Seed. The believer doesn't have to work in order to enter into the fullness found in Christ; he simply believes. What a blessing to be at rest! This world is such a restless, warring place. What little peace and rest it offers is a terrible counterfeit version of what God has for us.

> There remains therefore a rest for the people of God. For he who has entered His rest has himself also ceased from his works as God did from His.
> **Hebrews 4:9–10**

There remains a rest for the people of God. When Jesus died upon the cross at Calvary, He cried, "It is finished!" (John 19:30). He finished the work He came to do. Our salvation is based upon the finished work at Calvary. This is the place of rest for every believer. Christian believers don't keep the Old Testament Sabbath because that Sabbath was one of the shadows that Jesus came to fulfill. Our perfect rest now is not in a day, but in a Person. Jesus said:

> "Come to Me, all you who labor and are heavy laden, and I will give you rest. Take My yoke upon you and learn from Me, for I am gentle and lowly in heart, and you will find rest for your souls. For My yoke is easy and My burden is light."
> **Matthew 11:28–30**

Every believer has already entered into this rest by placing faith in Jesus Christ. Here is the place where we should be living life. Believers believe, and so find a place of rest. A place of peace. Matthew tells the story about the woman with a female disease (also Mark 5:25-34).

> And suddenly, a woman who had a flow of blood for twelve years came from behind and touched the hem of His garment. For she said to herself, "If only I may touch His garment, I shall be made well." But Jesus turned around, and when He saw her He said, "Be of good cheer, daughter; your faith has made you well." And the woman was made well from that hour.
> **Matthew 9:20–22**

The condition she lived in left her completely hopeless. She had been hemorrhaging for twelve long years. She was in a constant state of ceremonial uncleanness, according to the Law (Leviticus 15:19-25). Moreover, she experienced a constant drain of life, since the life is in the blood (Leviticus 17:11). She was poor, having spent everything for a cure. I'm sure she experienced loneliness, had a very low self-esteem, and was probably very weak. Cut off from society, she was ashamed, embarrassed, and probably felt totally unworthy even to be alive. One day, a very noisy crowd passed by her and she hid. She was unclean. But she heard what people were saying. Jesus of Nazareth was in their midst and He was healing people. This got her attention. She could feel their joy. She could feel life in that crowd! And then she saw Jesus as He was passing by. For her, this was the chance of a lifetime! She simply made up her mind, If only I may touch His garment, I shall be made well. No hype. No working herself into a frenzy. She simply believed if Jesus could do it for others, He could do it for her. When she made up her mind, she found settled peace. She would get her miracle. That's faith! It's that simple.

> Immediately the fountain of her blood was dried up, and she felt in her body that she was healed of the affliction. And Jesus, immediately knowing in Himself that power had gone out of Him, turned around in the crowd and said, "Who touched My clothes?" But His disciples said to Him, "You see the multitude thronging You, and You say, 'Who touched Me?'" And He looked around to see her who had done this thing. But the woman, fearing and trembling, knowing what had happened to her, came and fell down before Him and told Him the whole truth. And He said to her, "Daughter, your faith has made you well. Go in peace, and be healed of your affliction."
> **Mark 5:29–34**

Jesus said her faith made her well. Her faith drew virtue from Jesus. "Now faith is the substance of things hoped for, the evidence of things not seen" (Hebrews 11:1). Genuine faith can touch God. It can move God. There is peace within a person who has genuine faith. It didn't matter if this woman was unclean. When you have genuine faith, you no longer care about what others think of you; what they may say about you. All that matters is what is happening between you and Jesus. You have great peace within when you have faith.

When Jesus is healing people, they can't keep it to themselves. They get excited and are full of joy. We see this when Philip went to the city of Samaria – possibly the same city that the woman at the well came from. This would explain their openness to the Gospel.

> Then Philip went down to the city of Samaria and preached Christ to them. And the multitudes with one accord heeded the things spoken by Philip, hearing and seeing the miracles which he did. For unclean spirits, crying with a loud voice, came out of many who were possessed; and many who were paralyzed and lame were healed. And there was great joy in that city.
> **Acts 8:5–8**

Philip was a Walking Revival. Jesus was moving powerfully through him. As he preached the Gospel, people were drawn to him and his message. That message was confirmed with signs following. Jesus worked miracles through Philip as he was led by the Spirit of God and the people were being drawn to God because of the power that comes with that message. As they responded in faith and repented, they were brought back into relationship with God. That's revival!

> When they had crossed over, they came to the land of Gennesaret. And when the men of that place recognized Him, they sent out into all that surrounding region, brought to Him all who were sick, and begged Him that they might only touch the hem of His garment. And as many as touched it were made perfectly well.
> **Matthew 14:34–36**

Many times our faith in God has a natural flow. There's no turmoil or straining here. There is peace because we rest in faith! This is where we live life. God wants to bring us to this place in Him.

> Let us therefore be diligent to enter that rest, lest anyone fall according to the same example of disobedience. For the word of God is living and powerful, and sharper than any two-edged sword, piercing even to the division of soul and spirit, and of joints and marrow, and is a discerner of the thoughts and intents of the heart. And there is no creature hidden from His sight, but all things are naked and open to the eyes of Him to whom we must give account.
> **Hebrews 4:11–13**

ALL THINGS ARE POSSIBLE

The night Jesus walked on water (Matthew 14:22-33) we read about the disciples rowing a boat in the midst of the sea. The storm was quite severe as they constantly turned the boat into the waves and wind so as not to be overturned in the water. They were tossed. The winds of adversity blew hard against them. It takes a lot of strength to row a boat on a good day. But this was a storm at night. They were doing everything within their own power to survive. After a while, they didn't even know what direction they were headed. This is a good picture of a person without Christ in their life. Lost. In turmoil. Struggling. Sapped of all strength. What we do on our own may not be enough because the powers coming against us are far more powerful than we are. When it comes to eternal salvation, there's nothing we could possibly do in our own strength to make heaven our home. We fall short every time. We need God! We need faith in God!

Like the children of Israel in Egypt, it was a darkness that can be felt. Out of this darkness come the winds and waves of adversity. The person struggles constantly to stay afloat. They're worn down and have no direction in life. This is not a good place to be, in light of eternity. They are living by hope, fear, and unbelief rather than living by faith. It was Peter who stepped out in faith.

> And Peter answered Him and said, "Lord, if it is You, command me to come to You on the water." So He said, "Come." And when Peter had come down out of the boat, he walked on the water to go to Jesus. But when he saw that the wind was boisterous, he was afraid; and beginning to sink he cried out, saying, "Lord, save me!" And immediately Jesus stretched out His hand and caught him, and said to him, "O you of little faith, why did you doubt?" And when they got into the boat, the wind ceased.
>
> **Matthew 14:28–32.**

Faith and obedience brings us into the supernatural dimension of God. Everything now becomes possible. When you have faith, you have rest. The two go hand in hand.

THE ANOINTING

In the fall of 1974 I read the book, *Ever Increasing Faith* by Smith Wigglesworth. I was forever changed. It stirred the possibilities of God within me. It caused me to see the Scriptures in a whole new light. Through the eyes of faith. I wanted all my friends to go with me to every hospital and pray for the sick! I think I only made it to a couple of hospitals, but the seed had been sown. Since then, I have prayed for the sick in over fifty countries during a 45-year period and have seen many miracles of healing. This is a living reality for those who walk in faith. It is His life working through our life. We have a divine flow of resurrection life. We become a conduit of God's power. Whether it's eternal life, healing, or whatever you need to be delivered from, God, by His Holy Spirit, moves through you in power! This is what the Bible calls "the anointing." It is divine enablement. It was prevalent in the daily life of Christ. It's what made Him a Walking Revival wherever He went.

> And He was handed the book of the prophet Isaiah. And when He had opened the book, He found the place where it was written: "The Spirit of the LORD is upon Me, Because He has anointed Me To preach the gospel to the poor; He has sent Me to heal the brokenhearted, To proclaim liberty to the captives And recovery of sight to the blind, To set at liberty those who are oppressed; To proclaim the acceptable year of the LORD." Then He closed the book, and gave it back to the attendant and sat down. And the eyes of all who were in the synagogue were fixed on Him. And He began to say to them, "Today this Scripture is fulfilled in your hearing."
> **Luke 4:17–21**

One of the most powerful truth-filled stories in the Bible is the story of David and Goliath. But the story doesn't begin with David coming out against Goliath. It begins when he is anointed to be the next king of Israel.

> So it was, when they came, that he looked at Eliab and said, "Surely the LORD's anointed is before Him!" But the LORD said to Samuel, "Do not look at his appearance or at his physical stature, because I have refused him. For the LORD does not see as man sees; for man looks at the outward appearance, but the LORD looks at the heart." . . . And Samuel said to Jesse, "Are all the young men here?" Then he said, "There remains yet the youngest, and there he is, keeping the sheep." And Samuel said to Jesse, "Send and bring him. For we will not sit down till he comes here." So he sent and brought him in. Now he was ruddy, with bright eyes, and good-looking. And the LORD said, "Arise, anoint him; for this is the one!" Then Samuel took the horn of oil and anointed him in the midst of his brothers; and the Spirit of the LORD came upon David from that day forward.
> **1 Samuel 16:6–7, 11-13.**

As David is anointed the next king of Israel, you can already see the Seed of David at work. God sent a distressing spirit to trouble King Saul, who was backslidden. Saul's servants settled on David as the prime candidate to comfort King Saul. It's easy to see the hand of God behind this.

> But the Spirit of the LORD departed from Saul, and a distressing spirit from the LORD troubled him. And Saul's servants said to him, "Surely, a distressing spirit from God is troubling you. Let our master now command your servants, who are before you, to seek out a man who is a skillful player on the harp. And it shall be that he will play it with his hand when the distressing spirit from God is upon you, and you shall be well." So Saul said to his servants, "Provide me now a man who can play well, and bring him to me." Then one of the servants answered and said,

> "Look, I have seen a son of Jesse the Bethlehemite, who is skillful in playing, a mighty man of valor, a man of war, prudent in speech, and a handsome person; and the LORD is with him." Therefore Saul sent messengers to Jesse, and said, "Send me your son David, who is with the sheep." . . . And so it was, whenever the spirit from God was upon Saul, that David would take a harp and play it with his hand. Then Saul would become refreshed and well, and the distressing spirit would depart from him.
>
> **1 Samuel 16:14–19, 23**

But this was just the beginning of the Seed of David at work in his life. In obscurity, when no one was watching, David began growing in the anointing of God. He was tending his father's sheep when he was called into his father's house and anointed to be the next king of Israel. For a son, tending sheep was probably one of the lowest jobs in the household. Once anointed, he went right back to tending his father's sheep. Rather than getting puffed up and prideful, flaunting his new position over his brothers, he returned to the job he was doing when he was called. He was working when God called him and he went right back to working after God called him. When God calls a person to ministry, there is always a space of time before that person actually enters into the reality of that calling.

I attended my first Bible conference seven months after giving my life to Christ. At that time, the church had a congregation of 25-30, and a steady stream of people continued to come in and pray to get saved. I was doing most of the follow-up because all I knew is that I wanted everyone to get what I got. I wanted everyone to be saved. Everything I did was to learn more about Jesus and help others do the same. Every day, I was doing something for God. I had given Him my entire life. Nothing else mattered. I served in the local church any way I could.

On the Tuesday night service of that conference, the preacher preached on the call of God. I clearly sensed the call of God to be a minister of the Gospel of Jesus Christ. Once again I was at the altar, weeping before God in response to that high calling. To this day, I can still feel the moment of that calling. It became one of the major reference points in my life. I had entered God's school of preparation. Three years later, I was sent out to pioneer and pastor my first church. There was a lot of serving and learning during that period of time.

David spent his time learning the ways of God, from the moment God called him to the time he came into public ministry. God was teaching him how to tend his father's sheep in preparation for leading Israel, God's sheep. David learned in obscurity. No one was watching what God was doing in this young man's life. It was here that he learned faith in God. Later, he told King Saul about fighting a lion and a bear while taking care of the sheep. These were his credentials for taking on Goliath.

> But David said to Saul, "Your servant used to keep his father's sheep, and when a lion or a bear came and took a lamb out of the flock, I went out after it and struck it, and delivered the lamb from its mouth; and when it arose against me, I caught it by its beard, and struck and killed it. Your servant has killed both lion and bear; and this uncircumcised Philistine will be like one of them, seeing he has defied the armies of the living God." Moreover David said, "The LORD, who delivered me from the paw of the lion and from the paw of the bear, He will deliver me from the hand of this Philistine."
> **Samuel 17:34–37**

David, the man after God's own heart, addresses King Saul as "your servant." He was first and foremost a servant. David had a warrior-like faith stirring within him to take on Goliath. He was not afraid of Goliath. He was at peace before God and King Saul, knowing that he could take on this giant of a man like he had taken on the lion and the bear – because he had faith in God. He had developed his relationship with God in obscurity. Now his faith was taking him public. But none of this meant anything to David. All he could think of was this loud-mouthed giant of a soldier who was taunting the army of Israel.

Every Israeli soldier trembled with fear when they heard Goliath speak. Whenever you have fear, you will not have faith. The same words that stirred up fear in the soldiers stirred up faith in David. He was ready to rise up and conquer in the name of the Lord. As you grow in the anointing of God, you grow in faith. It takes faith to move in the anointing of God. Goliath didn't strike fear into David as he did with the others, because while alone before God, David had been made ready to take him on. He had been prepared when no one was watching. Because David had genuine faith in God, nothing else mattered. It did not matter to him who was or wasn't watching at that moment. His brothers were all there – trembling in fear just like the others. But not David.

When you move with God in faith, nothing else matters. At that moment, it is just you and God and the situation before you. No boasting goes on here. Only obedience to the stirring of God within you. It's just you and God and the situation. You don't have to work up some kind of faith frenzy. You rest in God because your faith in Him is real. David's testimony of the lion and the bear convinced King Saul to send him out against Goliath. Genuine God-given faith will open doors that no man can shut. When you have the heart of a servant and are anointed of God, you will not shake with fear; you will rise and conquer. As David went down the hill toward Goliath, he was serving God and serving Israel.

There is no fear in faith. Faith takes action and moves with God. As David raced toward Goliath, his eyes were locked upon the enemy. He wasn't looking around, unsure of himself or unsure of God. He charged forward in the assurance that God was with him and that together they were going to take care of Goliath. Satan is arrogant and loudmouthed. He is always taking to the battleground to thwart the purposes of God. For more than forty days, Goliath's words had stopped an entire army; God's army. The more he mouthed off, the more they trembled in fear. But then along came David. Anointed of God. No fear here, only faith. The moment David set out against Goliath in faith, he dominated the battleground. He turned it around in his favor. Goliath never saw it coming – just as Satan never saw that killing Jesus on the cross would play into the hands of the living God.

When Goliath challenged the entire army, you see Satan's wrath against the people of God; you see his ability to stop a multitude of God's people through fear. As David got closer to Goliath and he realized how young David was, he became very angry. Now his words targeted David personally. Look at this exchange:

> So the Philistine came, and began drawing near to David, and the man who bore the shield went before him. And when the Philistine looked about and saw David, he disdained him; for he was only a youth, ruddy and good-looking. So the Philistine said to David, "Am I a dog, that you come to me with sticks?" And the Philistine cursed David by his gods. And the Philistine said to David, "Come to me, and I will give your flesh to the birds of the air and the beasts of the field!" Then David said to the Philistine, "You come to me with a sword, with a spear, and with a javelin. But I come to you in the name of the LORD of hosts, the God of the armies of Israel, whom you have defied. This day the LORD will deliver you into my hand, and I will strike you and take your head from you. And this day I will give the carcasses of the camp of the Philistines to the birds of the air and the wild beasts of the earth, that all the earth may know that there is a God in Israel. Then all this assembly shall know that

> the LORD does not save with sword and spear; for the battle is the LORD's, and He will give you into our hands."
> **1 Samuel 17:41–47**

The demon-possessed warrior was no match for a godly warrior moving in faith by the anointing. Once again, no fear here; only faith. Even when the heat was turned up against David and the attack was coming against him personally, he was at rest in God. This is faith. Faith in God will always turn the battle. When God moves through a person, there's nothing the devil can do to stop Him.

> So it was, when the Philistine arose and came and drew near to meet David, that David hurried and ran toward the army to meet the Philistine. Then David put his hand in his bag and took out a stone; and he slung it and struck the Philistine in his forehead, so that the stone sank into his forehead, and he fell on his face to the earth. So David prevailed over the Philistine with a sling and a stone, and struck the Philistine and killed him. But there was no sword in the hand of David. Therefore David ran and stood over the Philistine, took his sword and drew it out of its sheath and killed him, and cut off his head with it.
> **1 Samuel 17:48–51**

David ran toward Goliath. No pride or arrogance in David. Only faith. Unbelievers and doubters always criticize people who move in faith, knowing that they themselves surely don't. Just another angle of attack from the enemy of our souls. When I spend time around those with not much faith, their attitude towards those that do have faith amazes me. They usually see them as arrogant or full of pride. After all is said and done, it always comes back to just you and God. Especially when it comes to moving in faith with God. As we move in faith, we rest in God. Faith is contagious: it affects all around us. And faith doesn't just stop at the immediate victory.

> And when the Philistines saw that their champion was dead, they fled. Now the men of Israel and Judah arose and shouted, and pursued the Philistines as far as the entrance of the valley and to the gates of Ekron.
> 1 Samuel 17:51–52

So powerful was the Spirit of God through David against Goliath that it caused the Philistine army to flee for their lives! As they fled, the Spirit of God moved upon the whole army of Israel – the same army that earlier had shaken with fear. They chased after the Philistines and God wrought a great victory through them that day. They had revival! David became a Walking Revival the moment he slew Goliath, triggering faith in others to believe God.

This same anointing caused many to gather to David while he was on the run from his father-in-law, King Saul. Many of these men became the mighty men of Israel – the Seed of David at work. God builds His Kingdom through us as relationships are built. David didn't send ambassadors to reach out to these men. They were drawn to him by the Spirit of God. I'm sure David was amazed that these men came to him. God did this.

> David therefore departed from there and escaped to the cave of Adullam. So when his brothers and all his father's house heard it, they went down there to him. And everyone who was in distress, everyone who was in debt, and everyone who was discontented gathered to him. So he became captain over them. And there were about four hundred men with him.
> 1 Samuel 22:1–2

God was establishing His Kingdom in Israel through David just as He'll use us to establish His Kingdom today through the building of His Church. Pastor, do you want more men in your church? God will bring them. All it takes is faith.

> So Jesus answered and said to them, "Have faith in God. For assuredly, I say to you, whoever says to this mountain, 'Be removed and be cast into the sea,' and does not doubt in his heart, but believes that those things he says will be done, he will have whatever he says. Therefore I say to you, whatever things you ask when you pray, believe that you receive them, and you will have them."
> **Mark 11:22–24**

Becoming a Walking Revival is God's business. Faith is at the very heart of this process, because everything in the Kingdom of God moves by faith.

> But without faith it is impossible to please Him, for he who comes to God must believe that He is, and that He is a rewarder of those who diligently seek Him.
> **Hebrews 11:6**

CHAPTER SIX

DISCIPLESHIP

And when He had called His twelve disciples to Him,
He gave them power.
Matthew 10:1

GOD'S METHOD

Even a light study of the four gospels will bring you to the conclusion that part of God's plan of redemption for the world hinges upon Jesus' method of evangelism. As I said before, Jesus could have overthrown Roman rule in Israel, but He didn't. The Jewish people were looking for a Messiah to come who would do that very thing. Jesus could have raised up an army to fight Rome. But He didn't. The real issue wasn't that Israel was occupied and ruled by an enemy nation. That was bad enough. But there was something far worse than that: the issue of sin. Sin controlled Israel more than the Roman army ever could. The Son of God came into this world to deal with our sin problem which was spiritual, not the Roman rule problem which was physical.

Jesus didn't come just to teach and preach. He came to make a deposit. He would pay a great price just to make this deposit by laying down His life on the earth as a ransom for many. He could have gathered the multitudes and had a national movement. But He didn't. What He did do was reach the individual. He was a Walking Revival. He would reach people, who would reach people, who would reach people. This is revival!

The very reason the Son of God came into this world was to bring the individual back into a right relationship with God the Father. Man, utterly sinful by nature, was dead to God. "And you He made alive, who were dead in trespasses and sins" (Ephesians 2:1). Unless God moved, we were lost for time and eternity. Jesus walked the earth sinless. He was the Innocent who came to die for us, the guilty. He was the only One who could do this. Jesus died on the cross at Calvary and then raised Himself from the dead so He could spiritually deposit Himself into those who would call upon His name and be saved.

By being born again, we are brought back into the right relationship with the living God which Adam once enjoyed. We are no longer dead to God through sin, but alive through Christ. His life was the ultimate sacrifice. He died so that we can live. He revived our relationship with God through His sacrifice.

How was His one life going to make a difference in reaching every person who was ever born since? He only walked the earth for 33 years before we crucified Him. And only three of those years were spent in public ministry. How could He possibly reach the world? What was His method?

The only method He used in reaching the lost was discipleship, and discipleship only works through relationship. Now we're back to the basics: Love God; Love People. His ministry was not to the masses, but to the individual. He didn't save entire groups, tribes, or nations. He saved individuals. There is no such thing as a Christian nation. But there are many Christians inside of nations, and many individuals reached through relationships. Discipleship is God's only method to reach the world. It worked then and it works today.

DISCIPLESHIP

This concept of discipleship was nothing new, even in Jesus' day. Several scriptures in the Old Testament speak of discipleship. Different translations bring this to our attention.

> Fifty disciples of the prophets stood at a distance as Elijah and Elisha stood by the Jordan River.
> **2 Kings 2:7 (GW)**
>
> The wife of one of the prophets' disciples pleaded with Elisha.
> **2 Kings 4:1 (Voice)**
>
> Disciples so often get into trouble; still, GOD is there every time.
> **Psalm 34:19 (MSG)**
>
> "And all your [spiritual] sons will be disciples [of the LORD], And great will be the well-being of your sons . . ."
> **Isaiah 54:13 (AMP)**

Discipleship was nothing new to the Jews. In the New Testament, we find that even the Pharisees had disciples.

> That's when the Pharisees plotted a way to trap him into saying something damaging. They sent their disciples, with a few of Herod's followers mixed in . . .
> **Matthew 22:15 (MSG)**
>
> They sent their disciples to Him, along with the Herodians . . .
> **Matthew 22:16 (AMP)**

It was common knowledge John the Baptist also had disciples:

> A synagogue leader came to Jesus while he was talking to John's disciples.
> **Matthew 9:18 (GW)**
>
> Jesus answered John's disciples, "Go back, and tell John what you hear and see: . . ."
> **Matthew 11:4 (GW)**

John's disciples were Jewish by birth and John had one message: repentance. He didn't preach anything beyond this. We read of the Jewish people (especially the Jewish leaders) saying to Jesus, "We are Abraham's family." They reveled in their Jewishness.

> Then Jesus said to those Jews who believed Him, "If you abide in My word, you are My disciples indeed. And you shall know the truth, and the truth shall make you free." They answered Him, "We are Abraham's descendants, and have never been in bondage to anyone. How can You say, 'You will be made free'?"
> **John 8:31–33**

The Jewish people of that day were in bondage in more ways than one. First, by birth: they lived their culture bound by the Mosaic Law. They were also under Roman rule. John the Baptist represented the old system, the Law. John's disciples most likely served by controlling the crowds and helping baptize people. Their discipleship was probably no deeper than this. They did not even have to be spiritual. They were Jewish; God's chosen people by birth. And they were servants. There was nothing wrong with their service. It was natural and it was commendable.

After Jesus was baptized by John, He created His own culture of discipleship. Before starting His public ministry, He gathered disciples to Himself. John and Andrew were the first. They had been John's disciples, but began following Jesus after He was baptized. Andrew then brought his brother, Peter. The next day, Jesus finds Philip on His way to Galilee, and Philip then finds Nathanael. Shortly after, Matthew was called to follow Jesus as He passed through Capernaum. Discipleship has everything to do with relationships, both vertical and horizontal. Jesus had gathered men to Himself and made them His disciples.

The culture of His disciples was through re-birth. You had to be born again to be discipled by Jesus. Jesus dealt with the inward man as He discipled them. It wasn't a one-dimensional discipleship like John's disciples had. Jesus went after the heart of these men and it touched every area of their lives. The carnal man cannot be discipled. To be a Jesus disciple means it has everything to do with the spiritual person. It has to do with Christ within, developing the spiritual man.

John the Baptist discipled men to prepare people for baptism. They served. All discipleship starts out in serving. Jesus' disciples were based on the culture of relationship. It had everything to do with the inward man. It taught on all things pertaining to life. It was spiritual. That's what discipleship is all about. Jesus, the Disciple-maker, constantly poured His life into these men: sharing things with them, making deposits. They, in turn, would ask questions to draw things out of Him. It all flowed through relationship.

Go to any church throughout the world and you will find people who serve. In a sense they are "John" disciples. They don't even have to be saved to serve that congregation. It's in their hearts to serve and that's what they do. It doesn't mean they're bad people, or that what they're doing is wrong. But you don't have to be very spiritual to serve in this capacity. They're given something to do and they do it out of the goodness of their hearts. At this stage, no one is necessarily putting things into their lives and they are probably not drawing things out of someone in order to do what they do. They may have relationship because they grew up in the church and this is all they've ever known. They serve as a natural outflow of their heart and it may not be too spiritual. But they serve.

In a church where there is a culture of discipleship, people generally have had a salvation experience with Christ and so it's in their hearts to serve. Both John disciples and Jesus disciples serve. The difference is that one person or several people are speaking into the lives of the Jesus disciple. They are growing spiritually because of it. They, on the other hand, are drawing things out of others in the congregation because of the hunger in their hearts to learn and to grow in God. They also see something in others that they want. Like Elisha with Elijah, they hang out so they can grab whatever they can. As these grow in God and serve, they become Christ's disciples. This happens by choice. No one forces them. It is a natural flow of life. It's as natural as a friendship. It is also supernatural. If it's real discipleship, it is centered in Christ.

THE NUTS AND BOLTS OF DISCIPLESHIP

A Walking Revival is a disciple-maker. They live their lives doing everything within their power to help others fulfill the will of God in their lives. "What can I do to help you?" This is what is in their hearts. This is what goes beyond just serving. There is the pouring of one's life into another while that other is drawing things out. We will grow in God because we want to. But we're still serving.

When I was saved, I only had two real reference points as to what a Christian should be like. One was the woman I worked with that had taken me to church, and the other was my pastor. I ended up seeing both almost every day for the first six months of my salvation. After a short time, I wanted whatever it was that my pastor had. He had been saved three years before at the beginning of the Jesus People Movement and he was on fire for God. He was moving with God! Because he was a Walking Revival, I became a Walking Revival!

When I got filled with the Holy Spirit, I worshiped God just like my pastor did, because I got what he had in the same way that he had it. I became the first song leader in the church. Everyone coming into our church saw the two of us on the platform worshipping God. Most of them were ignorant concerning the things of God, just as I had been. We prayed for people who got saved to be filled with the Spirit of God and they would be filled on the spot. One year after receiving Christ into my life, we had about 75 people in the church who were on fire for God, and the spirit of revival broke loose as we kept growing. It was so powerful! We wanted church every night. On the nights when there was no service, we would call each other up and say, "Let's go do something for God!" It was a church full of Walking Revivals and it was infectious! Our lives were impacting the lives of those we came in contact with. The entire church had an atmosphere of revival! The life of God through Christ in us was the most powerful thing happening! We were going to take the world for Jesus!

I learned to pray because I went to prayer meetings where often it was just the pastor and me. He would pray out loud and I would kind of pray silently along with him. He would say something and I would say, "Amen, Lord. Same here." As time passed, I began to pray for similar things. Without really realizing it, I was drawing things from my pastor. It was just a natural flow of life. He never told me, "I'm going to pray now. Pray like me." But he was imparting his spirit and vision to me without either of us realizing what was going on.

I would go with my pastor on outreaches to tell others about Jesus. I just mimicked what he did. It's all I knew. But that's how I learned. And something else developed inside me: a hunger for God. There was the giving; the impartation. And there was the hunger, causing me to draw the things of God toward me. It is in this realm where God truly begins working in us; where true discipleship takes place. It is always in the going, as He builds His Church through us. By the time I was sent out to pastor my first church, we had more than fifty men lined up who wanted to preach. We were experiencing a move of God! The Jesus People Movement was alive and well in our church. Because we were Walking Revivals, the others coming into the church became Walking Revivals, too. To us, this was normal Christianity.

As the church grew, I also became a person that others mimicked. It wasn't just my pastor any longer. It was him, me, and the others as they came in. We carried the same spiritual DNA, so to speak. Relationships were formed as the church grew. We were a community of believers. We became a culture of discipleship. We loved God and one another. We ministered to one another in the Lord. We were all going in the same direction, like the Early Church in Acts. We were all in one accord in one place (Acts 2:1). God did this. Then God really began pouring out His Spirit on our church, much like He had in the Book of Acts.

> So continuing daily with one accord in the temple, and breaking bread from house to house, they ate their food with gladness and simplicity of heart, praising God and having favor with all the people. And the Lord added to the church daily those who were being saved.
> **Acts 2:46–47**

I have experienced this same move of God everywhere I have pastored. As an evangelist, I experience much of the same thing wherever I go and preach. Why? Because of Christ in me is still working through me to build His Church. This is what real discipleship produces. I am a Walking Revival!

A CULTURE OF DISCIPLESHIP

In order to make disciples as a pastor, I became vulnerable to those I pastored; an open book. Why? Because I was an example for others to follow. If you're a pastor who wants more men in your church, become a disciple-maker. Become transparent to men about the things of God. Live your life asking, "What can I do to help you find and fulfill the will of God for your life?" Put yourself in this position and God will draw men to you.

Modern day John disciples live in a culture of service. Plugging in microphones. Running outreaches. Men may find themselves in a position which knocks the rough edges off their lives. Mentoring does this, but there is nothing too spiritual here. It's what the natural man can do. Even the unconverted can shine here. Every church has its servants.

Modern day Jesus disciples live in a culture of relationship. Serving is a part of this. But relationship is everything! It takes serving to another level. Relationship with God and man. This is the Kingdom of God! It's supernatural, because in real discipleship, Jesus is still the One discipling men! He's still the key to real discipleship. He still gets involved. This takes place through relationship. It happens by the Spirit of God.

There is a fine line between discipling men and controlling men. If you have "your" disciples, you have John disciples. You have created, in essence, "yes men" and you control all their serving. Churches are full of this kind of people. But if you have Jesus disciples, you will have everything that John disciples have plus a lot more. The bottom line is: if you're involved in genuine discipleship, these men are not "your" disciples. They belong to God. They're His disciples. The key to making Jesus disciples is that you've done all you can to help these men learn how to lay hold of God for themselves. They have pressed into God, and now they have developed their own genuine relationship with God through Jesus Christ. They are now disciples of Jesus and what we do in the natural begins to decrease so that Christ may increase in their lives. A man reaches a point in his life where he develops a genuine relationship with Jesus and begins to be led by the Spirit of God; the Spirit of Truth, whose business it is to reveal Christ in us and through us. This is where Jesus becomes the Chief Disciple-maker in a person's life. It is spiritual. It is supernatural. It is God at work.

THE TURNING POINT

Today Jesus is still the Disciple-maker. How can we, as ministers, help men to lay hold of God so that God can lay hold of them? Mainly through relationship. Drawing these men close to you, and creating an atmosphere of hunger for God through serving, Bible study, outreaches, and relationships. As you learn to be a giver, they will learn to draw things out of you. Take them with you. Spend time with them. Give them time to receive and grow in God through Christ and Him alone! These disciples belong to God, not to you or anyone else. Only God owns what He is doing.

John chapter 14 ends with Christ leading the disciples from the Passover in the upper room to their destination at the Garden of Gethsemane. The next two chapters record Christ giving to His disciples one last time as they walked toward Gethsemane. He uses the grapevine to describe Christian service and the need for a good relationship with Him if you're going to serve well. The key in John chapter 15 is the word abide. What abiding looks like in real life involves (most importantly) praying to Jesus and studying His Word. Relationship!

Real discipleship is a natural flow of life. It's not walking around speaking King James English to other men. It's not having a discipleship moment. It's simply a constant giving and drawing out through relationship that helps us reach the point of abiding in Christ. This is where real discipleship takes place. Jesus now becomes the Chief Discipler in your life. As Jesus was about to be arrested and crucified, He began teaching His disciples about life flow. Take time and study John 15. This is very powerful stuff! The fruit spoken about here comes through the building of His Church.

There is a turning point in every disciple's life where they transition from being a John disciple to becoming a Jesus disciple.

> "I've told you these things for a purpose: that my joy might be your joy, and your joy wholly mature. This is my command: Love one another the way I loved you. This is the very best way to love. Put your life on the line for your friends. You are my friends when you do the things I command you. I'm no longer calling you servants because servants don't understand what their master is thinking and planning. No, I've named you friends because I've let you in on everything I've heard from the Father."
> **John 15:11-15 (MSG)**

This is a transitional moment in the disciples' lives. Jesus speaks these words just hours before He is arrested and crucified. They've finished the Last Supper and Judas has already left to betray Him. Jesus is only speaking to the eleven. He tells them they are no longer servants (slaves), but now they're friends. This has everything to do with relationships, once again. An honest culture of discipleship in a church will bring each disciple to this point. The human disciple-maker cannot take them any further. Only God can bring the disciple into a relationship with Christ, where true discipleship begins. Jesus was about to depart planet Earth. They were going to have to live for Him without Him physically being with them.

By reaching this point in their relationship with Jesus, His disciples now had real personal communion with Him. Jesus is the Vine and we're the branches. God the Father is the Husbandman and the Holy Spirit is the flow of life! This is all supernatural! It is the divine flow of life from God the Father, through the Son, by the Holy Spirit, that makes us a Walking Revival. When you reach this place in your relationship with God, you are no longer seen as a servant. Now you are a friend. The key to all human discipleship is to get us to this point in our walk with God.

Friendship is here defined in terms of both revelation and imitation. Almost at the beginning of His ministry, Jesus said these words:

> Then Jesus answered and said to them, "Most assuredly, I say to you, the Son can do nothing of Himself, but what He sees the Father do; for whatever He does, the Son also does in like manner. For the Father loves the Son, and shows Him all things that He Himself does; and He will show Him greater works than these, that you may marvel. For as the Father raises the dead and gives life to them, even so the Son gives life to whom He will."
> **John 5:19–21**

Friendship is found in loving service. "Greater love has no one than this, than to lay down one's life for his friends" (John 15:13). Mutual love among Jesus' disciples doesn't stay within the community of disciples, but results in a mission to share it with the world. Remaining in Jesus (abiding) is defined as loving one another, and bearing fruit must be defined as reproducing oneself and one's spiritual relationship with Jesus in the lives of others. The evangelization of the world does not arise out of the disciples' conscious love or compassion for the world itself, nor for the masses of people in it, but out of their "in-house" love for each other. A single grain of wheat dies in order to produce many other grains; bringing forth, literally, "much fruit."

> "Most assuredly, I say to you, unless a grain of wheat falls into the ground and dies, it remains alone; but if it dies, it produces much grain."
> **John 12:24**
>
> "By this all will know that you are My disciples, if you have love for one another."
> **John 13:35**

Real discipleship has everything to do with relationships! Relationships with God and man, vertical and horizontal. Love God; Love People. This is the Kingdom of God.

> "As the Father hath loved me, so have I loved you."
> **John 15:9**

The human mind cannot fathom the greatness of the love of God the Father for God the Son. To compare His love for us to the Father's love for Him is to say that He loves us beyond human comprehension. Christ loved us when we were unlovable. Christ did not love us because of who we are but because of Who He is. We can honestly love others because of the love of Christ working through us. The Christ-like love between Christians is a fundamental value for effective outreach.

Fruit-bearing for God is not a human possibility; it is Christ's work through us. He is the Vine and we are the branches. As His life flows through us, we bear fruit. This is what a Walking Revival is all about. Jesus builds His Church through us. He's given us the keys of the Kingdom so we can build His Church! The turning point in any disciple's life is found here:

> "No longer do I call you servants, for a servant does not know what his master is doing; but I have called you friends, for all things that I heard from My Father I have made known to you."
> **John 15:15**

This is the place that God desires to see every Christian get to in their relationship with Him. This is the place where God is very real. Friends can openly speak to other friends without holding back. This is the power of genuine friendship. God wants this kind of relationship with us. It's the main reason Jesus came to die on the cross.

This life flow comes to us through Christ. The branches disconnected from the vine are good for nothing. Their only worth is to be pruned and burned. But if that branch is connected to the

Vine, the life flowing through it from God will produce much fruit – and that fruit will remain. How? Because the fruit has the seeds inside it to plant more vines, so that fruit goes on to produce perpetually. This is discipleship. It has everything to do with relationships. Not just a relationship as acquaintances, but as real friends. Only Christ can produce that depth of relationship.

When my wife and I raised our children, we considered our venture a success if by the time they turned 18 years of age they worked a job, had their own car for which they paid their own insurance, and could make it on their own if they moved out. As a pastor raising up disciples, we should consider the process successful when those disciples reach that turning point where Christ through the Holy Spirit becomes the One discipling them.

The Chief Discipler in my life for many years now has been Christ, because I reached that turning point with Him. I'm now able to clearly know and walk in the will of God. My pastor is still my pastor. When I get around him, I am always trying to draw something from him. I do the same with anyone else who crosses my path. I am still a disciple. I am Christ's disciple. I belong to Him and He belongs to me. We're friends. This is what makes me a Walking Revival: It's because He is a Walking Revival. This is the Christian life.

> And Jesus came and spoke to them, saying, "All authority has been given to Me in heaven and on earth. Go therefore and make disciples of all the nations, baptizing them in the name of the Father and of the Son and of the Holy Spirit, teaching them to observe all things that I have commanded you; and lo, I am with you always, even to the end of the age." Amen.
> **Matthew 28:18–20**

CHAPTER SEVEN

CROSS

"If anyone desires to come after Me, let him deny himself, and take up his cross, and follow Me."
Matthew 16:24

PRESENT DAY CHURCH

Christianity is not just another philosophy amongst many. Jesus is not just another God among many gods. He didn't come to earth, die on the cross, rise again the third day, ascend into heaven, and sit down at the right hand of the Father – just to give us another religion. He came, died, and resurrected to give us life, and that more abundantly (John 10:10). In order to be a Walking Revival in our short time on earth, we need to understand a few things.

The widespread lack of victorious living among believers is due to the fact that they can't discern the spiritual from the natural (carnal). The same people come to the altar every service, praying to be delivered from something. They pray or are led in a prayer of deliverance, and then assume the one prayer takes care of it all. Yet they are back praying for deliverance the next service, and the next; they are never truly delivered. They live in perpetual confusion, doubt, and unbelief because they are going to the altar in hope rather than in faith.

Churches today spend so much time and energy trying to be relevant to this present evil age that they have lost sight of the power of the Gospel. They work feverishly on their branding, trying to make the Gospel fit this generation rather than confronting this generation with the truth of the Gospel. Many church attendees go through religious motions but have never been born again. They look like Christians on the outside but lack something on the inside. Sadly, you can have a church life without a God life. Often people don't know the difference. Many churches are sincere in doing the best they can.

The preacher spends so much time defining life's problems that he has little or no time for the solution. Christ is hardly mentioned before he makes his appeal to people to give their lives to Jesus – if and when an altar call is given at all. The people are bewildered. Who is Jesus? What has He done for me? Why should I trust Him with my life? By and large, this preaching brings no conviction of sin by the Holy Spirit. No power is present to transform a life from darkness to light. No mention has been made of the victory that Christ purchased for us on Calvary's cross. People may feel remorse over actions as their emotions are manipulated by words, but they can only be convicted of sin by the power of the Holy Spirit of God.

The last words Jesus spoke on the cross were, "It is finished." It was and it is! He paid the price by dying so that we might live. This is the revelation we're to walk in. We're all sinners. We're all messed up. God knows all of this. We're not saved to walk in our messed up lives. We're saved to walk in the power of His resurrected life. As we grow in God we must learn to walk by faith, not by feelings; not by hope. We have an exchanged life! Live it! Live Christ daily!

The prevailing spiritual condition of the Last Days generation is alarming to say the least.

> But know this, that in the last days perilous times will come: For men will be lovers of themselves, lovers of money, boasters, proud, blasphemers, disobedient to parents, unthankful, unholy, unloving, unforgiving, slanderers, without self-control, brutal, despisers of good, traitors, headstrong, haughty, lovers of pleasure rather than lovers of God, having a form of godliness but denying its power. And from such people turn away!
> **Timothy 3:1–5**

There seems to be no distinction between the world and the church today. Rainbow flags drape churches where banners of compromise are proudly displayed: *We're all inclusive*; *Everyone is welcome here*; *Diversity*. In order to become relevant, they've lost their identity in Christ. They have an outward show of godliness but, by their very lifestyles, they deny the power of God. These churches, pushed around by the spirit of this present evil age, are based on feelings rather than faith. They identify now with the world, not with Christ. Social media has become the number one tool in the devil's arsenal to minimize the message of the Gospel of Christ and destroy an entire generation of youth. Oh, how we need Walking Revivals today! Great is the need for God to breathe upon this present generation which is *so lost!*

> I beseech you therefore, brethren, by the mercies of God, that you present your bodies a living sacrifice, holy, acceptable to God, which is your reasonable service. And do not be conformed to this world, but be transformed by the renewing of your mind, that you may prove what is that good and acceptable and perfect will of God.
> **Romans 12:1–2**

Real Christianity has to do with transformation. We've come out of darkness and into His marvelous light (1 Peter 2:9). The Church that Jesus is building is different than the world in which we live.

We're coming out of something to go into something new and different. If the Church is no different than the world, then when we go to church we're not getting saved and transformed; we're not moving from darkness into light – we're just changing dance partners.

HOW GOD CREATED MAN

Man, created by God, was created a triune being. He is a spirit, has a soul and dwells in a body. The body is what God has provided for man's soul and spirit to dwell in. It is the visible part of man. Our body has five senses. We can see, hear, smell, taste, and touch. It is through these five senses we become materialistically tied to this world. Our body is that which is most closely related to the earth. In fact, it is made of earth: made of clay. This is where the lust of the flesh, and the lust of the eyes, and the pride of life will have their outworking.

> For all that is in the world, the lust of the flesh, and the lust of the eyes, and the pride of life, is not of the Father, but is of the world.
> **1 John 2:16**

Man is a spirit. The body is visible but the spirit is invisible. It is the human spirit which is separate from the soul. But like the soul, it is immortal. Both will leave the body at death.

> Now may the God of peace Himself sanctify you completely; and may your whole spirit, soul, and body be preserved blameless at the coming of our Lord Jesus Christ.
> **1 Thessalonians 5:23**

It is the spirit of man that separates us from the animals. Only man has a spirit, capable of communicating with his Creator. It is only through his spirit that man can connect with God's Spirit to worship the Father who made him, loved him, and redeemed him.

> For we are the circumcision, who worship God in the Spirit, rejoice in Christ Jesus, and have no confidence in the flesh,
> **Philippians 3:3**

Man's spirit is in a state of perpetual death. It remains in utter darkness until it's redeemed. The spirit of man has the capacity to receive life (light).

> This is the message which we have heard from Him and declare to you, that God is light and in Him is no darkness at all. If we say that we have fellowship with Him, and walk in darkness, we lie and do not practice the truth. But if we walk in the light as He is in the light, we have fellowship with one another, and the blood of Jesus Christ His Son cleanses us from all sin.
> **1 John 1:5-7**

> And you He made alive, who were dead in trespasses and sins, in which you once walked according to the course of this world, according to the prince of the power of the air, the spirit who now works in the sons of disobedience, among whom also we all once conducted ourselves in the lusts of our flesh, fulfilling the desires of the flesh and of the mind, and were by nature children of wrath, just as the others. But God, who is rich in mercy, because of His great love with which He loved us, even when we were dead in trespasses, made us alive together with Christ (by grace you have been saved), and raised us up together, and made us sit together in the heavenly places in Christ Jesus, that in the ages to come He might show the exceeding riches of His grace in His kindness toward us in Christ Jesus. For by grace you have been saved through faith, and that not of yourselves; it is the gift of God, not of works, lest anyone should boast. For we are His workmanship, created in Christ Jesus for good works, which God prepared beforehand that we should walk in them.
> **Ephesians 2:1-10**

> Jesus answered, "Most assuredly, I say to you, unless one is born of water and the Spirit, he cannot enter the kingdom of God.

> That which is born of the flesh is flesh, and that which is born of the Spirit is spirit."
> **John 3:5-6**
>
> Therefore, if anyone is in Christ, he is a new creation; old things have passed away; behold, all things have become new.
> **2 Corinthians 5:17**

When you are redeemed by the blood of the Lamb, you have the light of life dwelling within you. You become a new creation. Our need today is to learn how to live daily as a new creation. We need to walk in this. Why? Because of the soul of man.

Man has a soul. This is the third part of man. The soul determines the motivation of the total person. Basically, the soul consists of mind, emotion and will. The mind of man is related to his learning capacity. Our mind is constantly fed thoughts, ideas and impressions, and then it accumulates, analyzes and files these away for future use. That's why it's so important that the mind be given material which will edify us spiritually.

Emotions (feelings) are what moves our will. Along with the mind, emotions seek to influence the will into complying with all the body's requests. Natural man is almost completely controlled by his emotions. Influenced by the mind and emotions, the will analyzes the facts fed into the mind and determines the direction the soul will take in either aligning itself with the spirit or the body. The will controls the mental and emotional behavioral patterns, which determine our choices in life.

It is the soul which stands before God morally responsible for the position we take in regard to the salvation provided for us by God through Christ on Calvary. Our soul is faced with the eternal decision.

> "And if it seems evil to you to serve the LORD, choose for yourselves this day whom you will serve, whether the gods which your fathers served that were on the other side of the River, or the gods of the Amorites, in whose land you dwell. But as for me and my house, we will serve the LORD."
> **Joshua 24:15**

The body is man's earthly, visible part, the part people can see. The spirit is the part of us which, though born dead in sin, can be made alive to communicate with and worship God. The soul is composed of mind, will, and emotion. It is the part of man which controls his eternal destiny. The body is related to the world, the spirit to God, and the soul to self. Understanding this will make all the difference in learning to live life as a new creation.

The natural man's relationship is with the world, sin, and Satan. The chief motivating force in the unsaved is "I." All of our existence is centered upon ourselves. We're the result of Adam's fall and we have Adam's fallen nature. Without Christ, we're alienated from the presence of God. It's not until our soul is awakened to our lost condition that we have any desire to be reinstated in a right relationship with our Maker.

> Jesus therefore answered and said to them, "Do not murmur among yourselves. No one can come to Me unless the Father who sent Me draws him; and I will raise him up at the last day."
> **John 6:43–44**

The natural man lives under the control of his fleshly appetites. The sinner is first body, then soul, and at last, the spirit. This is the direct opposite of the order God intended.

> But the natural man does not receive the things of the Spirit of God, for they are foolishness to him; nor can he know them, because they are spiritually discerned.
> **1 Corinthians 2:14**

The word natural in this verse is from a Greek word which describes the brute nature of people who are governed by their lust for sexual passion, fulfilling their lustful appetites. These people live for the present. A person who feels that nothing is more important than the satisfaction of their sexual urges cannot understand the meaning of chastity. A person who believes that the gathering of material things is the supreme goal in life cannot understand generosity and living for others. Never looking beyond worldly possessions, they cannot understand the things of God. They don't receive or embrace spiritual matters because they seem foolish to them. Unsaved people don't understand spiritual matters because they have no spiritual discernment. Until the Spirit of God draws them and they are convicted of sin, they will never come to the saving knowledge of Jesus Christ. Without this transformational conversion experience, they will never understand Christianity. They are simply on the outside looking in.

The natural man has no spiritual values. Spiritually, he walks in utter darkness and cannot know God. When people read the Bible with their natural eyes, they receive only natural knowledge. The deep things of Scripture are hidden from them because their spirit is dead. It is only through the spirit can a person really come into a knowledge of God. Natural man has no knowledge of God. He is an enemy of God and has no love for Him (James 4:4). He will not worship God because he lacks fear and faith in a supreme being. "The fear of the Lord is the beginning of wisdom" (Proverbs 9:10). The natural man refuses to receive God's truth or obey the Gospel of our Lord Jesus Christ.

> But if you have bitter envy and self-seeking in your hearts, do not boast and lie against the truth. This wisdom does not descend

> from above, but is earthly, sensual, demonic. For where envy and self-seeking exist, confusion and every evil thing are there.
> **James 3:14-16**

James lists the characteristics of natural man's wisdom. Unsaved people have bitter envy and strife in their hearts and think nothing of lying against truth; even boasting in doing so. Their thinking is earthly. They're so concerned about this temporal life that eternal life is given no consideration. Verse 15 says their thinking is devilish; demon-inspired. Jesus accused the Jews of His day of being liars and He said they were of their father, the devil! James goes on to say in verse 16 that natural man's wisdom results in confusion and every evil work. This is the condition of fallen man.

> For those who live according to the flesh set their minds on the things of the flesh, but those who live according to the Spirit, the things of the Spirit. For to be carnally minded is death, but to be spiritually minded is life and peace. Because the carnal mind is enmity against God; for it is not subject to the law of God, nor indeed can be. So then, those who are in the flesh cannot please God. But you are not in the flesh but in the Spirit, if indeed the Spirit of God dwells in you. Now if anyone does not have the Spirit of Christ, he is not His. And if Christ is in you, the body is dead because of sin, but the Spirit is life because of righteousness. But if the Spirit of Him who raised Jesus from the dead dwells in you, He who raised Christ from the dead will also give life to your mortal bodies through His Spirit who dwells in you. Therefore, brethren, we are debtors—not to the flesh, to live according to the flesh. For if you live according to the flesh you will die; but if by the Spirit you put to death the deeds of the body, you will live.
> **Romans 8:5-13**

Here, Paul contrasts the natural man (the flesh) and the spiritual man. He says the flesh is carnally minded and at enmity with God; completely dominated by sin.

> Now the works of the flesh are evident, which are: adultery, fornication, uncleanness, lewdness, idolatry, sorcery, hatred, contentions, jealousies, outbursts of wrath, selfish ambitions, dissensions, heresies, envy, murders, drunkenness, revelries, and the like; of which I tell you beforehand, just as I also told you in time past, that those who practice such things will not inherit the kingdom of God.
> **Galatians 5:19-21**

Here Paul lists the works of the flesh. In verse 21 he says that "they who practice such things will not inherit the kingdom of God." Let's look at this a little further in the Word of God.

> For what I am doing, I do not understand. For what I will to do, that I do not practice; but what I hate, that I do. If, then, I do what I will not to do, I agree with the law that it is good. But now, it is no longer I who do it, but sin that dwells in me. For I know that in me (that is, in my flesh) nothing good dwells; for to will is present with me, but how to perform what is good I do not find. For the good that I will to do, I do not do; but the evil I will not to do, that I practice. Now if I do what I will not to do, it is no longer I who do it, but sin that dwells in me. I find then a law, that evil is present with me, the one who wills to do good. For I delight in the law of God according to the inward man. But I see another law in my members, warring against the law of my mind, and bringing me into captivity to the law of sin which is in my members. O wretched man that I am! Who will deliver me from this body of death?
> **Romans 7:15-24**

Paul describes the inward battle he has with the natural man. Notice the self-centeredness of the natural man, putting stress on the personal pronoun "I." In verse 24, he sums up the predicament of the natural man as a wretched man in a body of death – one in definite need of deliverance. This is honesty. The struggle between the old man and the new man is constant. Our original thought is that the natural man is one whose spirit is dead to God. The unregenerate soul has taken the place of the spirit in their body as supreme ruler of man's earthly and eternal destiny. Without Christ, we are dead to God. In order to be a Walking Revival we're going to have to die a death: the death of the cross.

THE CROSS

Just going to church will not get you to heaven, but being born again will. Being born again is a miracle from God. We can't do this on our own. That's what the cross is all about. To put a person to death on a cross always takes two people. One person cannot crucify himself; it takes two. When we're in Christ, He is the other person. We can't live this Christian life without Him. After Jesus revealed that He would build His Church, He immediately began talking about the cross. He told His disciples He must go to Jerusalem and suffer many things at the hands of the elders and chief priests and scribes, and be killed, and be raised the third day (Matthew 16:21). Peter pulled Jesus aside and rebuked Him. "But He turned and said to Peter, 'Get behind Me, Satan! You are an offense to Me, for you are not mindful of the things of God, but the things of men'" (Matthew 16:23).

> Then Jesus said to His disciples, "If anyone desires to come after Me, let him deny himself, and take up his cross, and follow Me. For whoever desires to save his life will lose it, but whoever loses his life for My sake will find it. For what profit is it to a man if he gains the whole world, and loses his own soul? Or what will a man give in exchange for his soul?"
> **Matthew 16:24–26**

The believer who understands these two lives (and realizes the need in his own carnal life) will seek a remedy. That remedy is the cross. The old man – the flesh, self, natural man, or whatever you wish to call him – must be nailed to the cross. If self is on the cross, Jesus is on the throne. If self is still on the throne, Christ is on the cross. Self must step down and let Christ be enthroned before a believer can come into a right relationship with God. We must learn to put to death the flesh with all its desires and lusts (Galatians 5:24). The arena of the cross is where we put the old nature to death. This is where we fight. The natural man fights against the spirit to maintain this old flesh at any cost – all because we don't understand what God is doing.

When somebody speaks unkindly to you or cuts you down with a word, you want to strike back or run away and hide to nurse your wound until it becomes animosity. But as the cross is laid upon us, there is a lot of dying going on. The cross is bearing upon us to bring the old nature into surrender because God has a new life that you're going to live. "Yet not I, but Christ liveth in me" (Galatians 2:20).

> Therefore put to death your members which are on the earth: fornication, uncleanness, passion, evil desire, and covetousness, which is idolatry. Because of these things the wrath of God is coming upon the sons of disobedience, in which you yourselves once walked when you lived in them.
> **Colossians 3:5-7**

> For if you live according to the flesh you will die; but if by the Spirit you put to death the deeds of the body, you will live. For as many as are led by the Spirit of God, these are sons of God. For you did not receive the spirit of bondage again to fear, but you received the Spirit of adoption by whom we cry out, "Abba, Father." The Spirit Himself bears witness with our spirit that we are children of God, and if children, then heirs – heirs of God and joint heirs with Christ, if indeed we suffer with Him, that we may also be glorified together.
> **Romans 8:13-17**

In order to be a Walking Revival, we need to seek after spiritual knowledge, which will help the believer to reckon himself as dead to sin and alive to Christ (Romans 6:11). We need to understand that as we feed the spiritual man, Christ will grow on the inside. The greater our prayer life and study of the Word, and the more we assemble together with the Body of Christ, the greater will the work of the cross be inside us, bringing surrender to the old nature – the flesh, which is at enmity with God.

We're to pick up our cross daily and follow Christ. Which cross do you live? There were two thieves being crucified with Jesus that day. Both were guilty. One cursed God and the other honestly and openly confessed his sin and asked for mercy. One chose to hate God, rejecting grace; the other asked for salvation. By acknowledging his sin and being honest before God, he made heaven his home that day. He didn't earn it. He received it. It was a gift. He had faith. He chose to believe. Are you dying to live, or living to die? These are the two roads in life on which we can choose to travel. Either way, Christ is the center of it all. If we die to self, we also live Christ.

TRIALS

Early on in my Christian walk, I came to the conclusion that some of the trials and testing that I went through weren't so much for my benefit, but for others. God was preparing me for the ministry. What I needed was first-hand answers for other people's problems and questions. As I've grown older in the Lord, I've come to the conclusion that my years of trials and testing are for a far greater reason.

Jesus, hidden from the world around Him, lived a seemingly normal life until the developing life within Him reached maturity and He was ready to begin His ministry. As the seed of the new life is sown inside you, it is hidden away until it's revealed to you through circumstances, little by little, as you grow in Christ. The new life inside you is developing until a moment comes when God is ready to expose it to the world around you. You blink your eyes or wake up one day and everything has changed. God is now moving through your life for all the world to see. But what do they see? A Walking Revival. You're now someone God is moving through in a powerful way and you, along with those around you, stand back and say, "Look what God has done!"

God caused the seed to be planted within you and He knows how to water that seed through many circumstances. He knows how to get you away from busy paths. He might put you on the backside of a desert like He did with Moses. He might put you in places where you never dreamed you would be. It may take years for you realize what God is doing; before you have understanding. But you're no longer living under the fear and the domination of the spirit of the world. You know that God is at work developing you. You can now bear anything, as long as you know it is God.

One day, I woke up and realized it was God working behind everything I was going through to destroy the many things that I was doing. I could easily point my finger at this person for what they did to me, or that person who said this about me; or the many circumstances I faced in life in which I could easily make a case against someone or something. But behind all of this was God moving and applying the cross to my life. Things had to die in me so He could live! More than that, so He could move through me and build His Church. Now, I can now honestly say with David, "Yea, though I walk through the valley of the shadow of death, I will fear no evil; for You are with me; Your rod and Your staff, they comfort me" (Psalm 23:4). I am no longer just passing off religious information to people. I've become a Walking Revival. God now moves through me! Sometime after Paul was saved he had this great revelation:

> Yet indeed I also count all things loss for the excellence of the knowledge of Christ Jesus my Lord, for whom I have suffered the loss of all things, and count them as rubbish, that I may gain Christ and be found in Him, not having my own righteousness, which is from the law, but that which is through faith in Christ, the righteousness which is from God by faith; that I may know Him and the power of His resurrection, and the fellowship of His sufferings, being conformed to His death,
> **Philippians 3:8–10**

Paul realized how greatly Jesus had suffered at the hands of His creation after leaving the glory of heaven to walk amongst us and face everything thrown at Him – yet He was without sin. Paul faced so much in being a Walking Revival. He knew what it was to suffer.

> Are they Hebrews? So am I. Are they Israelites? So am I. Are they the seed of Abraham? So am I. Are they ministers of Christ? – I speak as a fool – I am more: in labors more abundant, in stripes above measure, in prisons more frequently, in deaths often. From the Jews five times I received forty stripes minus one. Three times I was beaten with rods; once I was stoned; three times I was shipwrecked; a night and a day I have been in the deep; in journeys often, in perils of waters, in perils of robbers, in perils of my own countrymen, in perils of the Gentiles, in perils in the city, in perils in the wilderness, in perils in the sea, in perils among false brethren; in weariness and toil, in sleeplessness often, in hunger and thirst, in fastings often, in cold and nakedness – besides the other things, what comes upon me daily: my deep concern for all the churches. Who is weak, and I am not weak? Who is made to stumble, and I do not burn with indignation? If I must boast, I will boast in the things which concern my infirmity. The God and Father of our Lord Jesus Christ, who is blessed forever, knows that I am not lying. In Damascus the governor, under Aretas the king, was guarding the city of the Damascenes with a garrison, desiring to arrest me; but I was let down in a basket through a window in the wall, and escaped from his hands.
> **2 Corinthians 11:22–33.**

Peter had experienced a similar revelation through his trials and testing. All for what purpose? That Christ may be glorified as He builds His Church through us.

> Beloved, do not think it strange concerning the fiery trial which is to try you, as though some strange thing happened to you; but rejoice to the extent that you partake of Christ's sufferings, that when His glory is revealed, you may also be glad with exceeding joy. If you are reproached for the name of Christ, blessed are you, for the Spirit of glory and of God rests upon you. On their part He is blasphemed, but on your part He is glorified. But let none of you suffer as a murderer, a thief, an evildoer, or as a busybody in other people's matters. Yet if anyone suffers as a Christian, let him not be ashamed, but let him glorify God in this matter.
> 1 Peter 4:12–16.

You may ask, Why am I going through this? Why is God allowing this to happen? Doesn't God really care? When the life of the Father, through the Son, has been planted into your spirit, you have what the whole world is looking for. You may not realize it upon first being converted to Christ, because it has not yet been developed to the level God intends it to be. You're a babe in Christ first, then you grow. In the growing experience there will be many crosses to endure. When God gives you a spiritual revelation, He has to work it out in you. He does this through trials. From the moment God saves you, the Holy Spirit begins to take you somewhere. He's giving you a reason to live; a reason to exist.

As this life of Christ within you is developed, it has one purpose: to reach out to those in need. His life swallows up death. The purpose of His life within you is to overcome all the death Adam put upon the human race. It's like a flashlight dispelling the darkness. Darkness never puts out the light. Light puts out the darkness.

Jesus is a revelation. In secular education we start from the outside and work in. But the knowledge of Christ starts from the inside and works out. Your mind has to grasp the truth which comes through your spirit. As we grow and develop in the grace and knowledge of our Lord Jesus Christ, we are led by the Spirit of Truth which teaches us all things. This is the Light that dispels the darkness.

When you enter into the fullness of the relationship with God that Jesus died for, you enter into really knowing who you are and Who He is. You really do know God now. You live and talk differently. Words like impossible will melt away from your speech. You know Who is backing you up and Who is within you. Wherever you go, Jesus goes with you. He Who is in you is what the whole world is begging for. They just don't know it. They may not even be looking for it. Yet, Christ is in you and you in Christ!

This miracle of the imparted life of Christ is far beyond our comprehension. Only God can reveal it. Within you is the Hope of the Ages. The Jews longed for their Messiah, but you have the Messiah living within you. They rejected Him because they thought He would come as a conqueror, but he was born in a manger. God's approach to man has always been in humility. The revelation of this life in Christ can come gradually or suddenly – it doesn't make any difference. But it will come. You can know truth but still not fully understand it. Only the Holy Spirit can reveal it to your heart. Remember, if you stay with it, your whole life will be different.

After 37 years of ministry, I woke up one day to find that my whole world had changed. Almost overnight, churches were canceling my revival meetings with no explanation or reason – and no new bookings were on the horizon. I'd never experienced anything like this before: in all my years, I'd had just five revivals cancel. It seems the churches were gravitating toward the next generation of younger preachers. Older guys like me, regardless of greater experience, were no longer in demand. I hadn't prepared for this. While we certainly should always look forward to the next generation in our vision to reach the lost – I simply hadn't seen this coming.

Most of my ministry involved working with the underbelly of society; dealing with those folks that most churches do not want to deal with. I wasn't wealthy. I had no savings. I basically lived from paycheck to paycheck during those years of ministry. Susan and I started carpooling to church with a friend because we couldn't even afford gas. That alone lasted for three years. I prayed constantly. I cried out to God. I went over my past looking for something that I did to warrant these deep trials. I looked at those around me to see if anything they did to me or said about me was to blame so I could point the finger at them.

Up until now, I had basically only experienced victory. Yes, I had some trials through the years, but nothing like this. This got deep. This lasted several years. I began to question many things before God. At times during this season I reached the point where I cried out, "Lord, if You're through with me, just take me home! I've nothing else to live for!"

After about five years with no let-up, I began to realize that behind every trial and heartache that I encountered, there was the hand of God. I can honestly say with David, "Yea, though I walk through the valley of the shadow of death, I will fear no evil; for You are with me; Your rod and Your staff, they comfort me" (Psalm 23:4). Could I blame God? In one sense, I could. He was behind all that I was going through. Why? The cross.

As I said before, no one can crucify themselves. It takes two people. As we pick up our cross daily, He is that second Person. Deep inside I knew the Scriptures and what it means to be in Christ. I also knew I was not at the place that He wanted me to be in

Christ – that supernatural place. I can't get there by myself. I need His help. But over those nine years, His help wasn't fun. The cross is never fun. It was never meant to be. It's death: death to self; death to the carnal mind. It is all for the furtherance of the Gospel; getting us ready to go into all the world.

Do you have a vision for the lost? Then get ready for the cross. Do you want to be a Walking Revival? It will cost you. It will cost everything you have and everything you are. Oh, that we may decrease that He may increase in our lives! This is what John the Baptist lived. Once Jesus was baptized, John (representing the Law) decreased, and Jesus (representing Grace) increased. Remember, in all you go through, God will not alter your personality. Your personality is you. God moves through human personality. As He gets deeper within you, the more Christ is seen by those around you. You become a magnet for the lost, the hurting, the down-trodden and depressed. They will gravitate toward you. Why? Because they sense you have the answers for their needs. This is where the power of God is found. This is the place of true humility. In the end it is worth it. No one likes getting there.

What we go through as we grow in Christ and pick up our cross daily is meant to bring us into a closer relationship with God. With the cross, sometimes the death is slow in coming and other times it can be sudden. God deals with us individually. Some growth may take years and other growth may take months or even weeks. He has a plan. He has a will. If the temperature is turned up in your life, it is for a reason. Some things in life need depth in the relationship. God has His reasons why. Ours is to surrender and submit; to be obedient. He will do the rest. It's His Kingdom. We're His creation. God knows what He is doing.

You can learn to live His life daily by faith: the resurrected life! Though you were dead in trespasses and sins, you are made alive through Christ! "And you He made alive, who were dead in trespasses and sins" (Ephesians 2:1). Live for God from this perspective, and you're on your way to becoming a Walking Revival!

CHAPTER EIGHT

SUPERNATURAL

"But you shall receive power when the Holy Spirit has come upon you; and you shall be witnesses to Me . . ."
Acts 1:8

THE HOLY SPIRIT

Some things never change. God never changes. The fact that people are born into this world having a sinful nature never changes, thus all are sinners. God's Word never changes. His Word, already spoken, will judge us on the day we come before God in that great court session in heaven. The Holy Spirit and fire is always on the move and that never changes. Entrance into the Kingdom of God by being saved through grace by faith never changes, either. But after we've been born from above, we constantly change.

Just as we identify with Christ in His death and resurrection through water baptism, Christ is identified with us by the baptism of the Holy Spirit. Now I have to admit, I live for the day God moves! I believe in God-sent revival. I believe Jesus moves through people to build His Church. I believe that I am – and that any child of God can become – a Walking Revival.

All of us come from different walks of life. Some have been taught about the infilling of the Holy Spirit. Others have just heard about it. Still others have been taught against it, saying it is of the devil. There's a whole cross-section of negatives and positives.

But regardless of what people say, it is very hard to dispute the reality of an experience. Once you have it, nothing bothers you. You just keep moving on and into all that God has for you. When you're filled with the Holy Spirit, you probably say, "God, how could there be anything more?" But there is.

Being filled with the Holy Spirit makes Jesus real to you and to those around you as He moves through your life. Just remember: as He begins working in your life, you're still in kindergarten. It's not long before God starts changing things in your life. He is never satisfied with you where you're at. If you ever think things are perfect and you have no problems, just keep looking over your shoulder.

It's the work of the Holy Spirit to see that the life of Christ in you has full expression through your life. Let me give you some advance warning. When the cross of Christ is laid on your life, you're going to struggle. You're going to be aggravated, and you're going to try to find something to satisfy the carnal nature so it won't die. When you pick up your cross daily, this struggle may come right away, or it may come five years down the road. But it will come. No one escapes it if they are truly seeking the indwelling Christ.

You can fight it all you want, or argue against it all you want; condemn it, justify it or blame it – but God won't let up! So rather than fight it, just accept it. "I don't want this," you say, but it's too late – you've already been awakened to it. You've got to go through God's processes if you want to be used by Him.

> From that time many of His disciples went back and walked with Him no more. Then Jesus said to the twelve, "Do you also want to go away?" But Simon Peter answered Him, "Lord, to whom shall we go? You have the words of eternal life. Also we have come to believe and know that You are the Christ, the Son of the living God."
> **John 6:66–69**

Jesus had been teaching some strong words about what it would take to follow Him. He claimed to be one with God and was pointing to His death as the way to life. His whole life had been a supernatural life. His birth, life, and miracles were all supernatural. His death on the cross was supernatural. His resurrection and bodily ascension into heaven was supernatural.

But there was more to His life (and thus also to ours) than just being supernatural. He went on to explain the spiritual nature of things: "It is the spirit that quickeneth; the flesh profiteth nothing: the words that I speak unto you, they are spirit, and they are life" (John 6:63). His words to Nicodemus were, "That which is born of the flesh is flesh; and that which is born of the Spirit is spirit" (John 3:6). His words are life-giving and they are spirit. They can quicken (make alive) because they impart the life of God. It's His Spirit in our spirit that imparts eternal life, the Seed of Christ which resides by His Word.

After this, some of Jesus' followers did walk away. Not only did they cease following Him, but they gave up whatever they had received from Him. They went back to their old ways of life because His teaching had sifted them. But at least the twelve remained. He continued putting them to the test. "Will you also go away?" He asked. But Peter had a revelation of the truth Jesus was speaking and said, "Lord, to whom shall we go? You have the words of eternal life. And we believe and are sure that You are the Christ, the Son of the living God" (John 6:68-69).

The time Jesus had with His disciples was coming to an end. They were still at the Last Supper and Judas had already left to betray Him. Jesus was hours away from being arrested and crucified; He was coming up to His cross. Little did the disciples know they also were about to face their own crosses. They were about to graduate from kindergarten. But Jesus wasn't going to leave them on their own. He was not going to leave them as orphans. He was going to give them something to live by without His physical presence among them. He would come to them by the Holy Spirit, the Spirit of Truth in which He had also walked during His time on this earth.

> "Most assuredly, I say to you, he who believes in Me, the works that I do he will do also; and greater works than these he will do, because I go to My Father. And whatever you ask in My name, that I will do, that the Father may be glorified in the Son. If you ask anything in My name, I will do it. "If you love Me, keep My commandments. And I will pray the Father, and He will give you another Helper, that He may abide with you forever – the Spirit of truth, whom the world cannot receive, because it neither sees Him nor knows Him; but you know Him, for He dwells with you and will be in you. I will not leave you orphans; I will come to you."
> **John 14:12–18**

After dying on the cross and rising from the dead, Jesus met with the disciples during a forty-day period. In Acts chapter 1, we read that He ascended into heaven. Just before His ascension, He spoke to them about being endued with power from on high.

> And being assembled together with them, He commanded them not to depart from Jerusalem, but to wait for the Promise of the Father, "which," He said, "you have heard from Me; for John truly baptized with water, but you shall be baptized with the Holy Spirit not many days from now." Therefore, when they had come together, they asked Him, saying, "Lord, will You at this time restore the kingdom to Israel?" And He said to them, "It is not for you to know times or seasons which the Father has put in His own authority. But you shall receive power when the Holy Spirit has come upon you; and you shall be witnesses to Me in

> Jerusalem, and in all Judea and Samaria, and to the end of the earth."
> **Acts 1:4–8**

Jesus told them to stay in Jerusalem until they were endowed with power. They knew God was going to move. They just didn't know when or how He was going to do it. But they knew He was going to move. So they obeyed. They stayed in Jerusalem. Daily they gathered together in the Upper Room and prayed. They sought God. Their idea of waiting on God was a prayer meeting. Then on the Day of Pentecost, something happened. God moved!

> When the Day of Pentecost had fully come, they were all with one accord in one place. And suddenly there came a sound from heaven, as of a rushing mighty wind, and it filled the whole house where they were sitting. Then there appeared to them divided tongues, as of fire, and one sat upon each of them. And they were all filled with the Holy Spirit and began to speak with other tongues, as the Spirit gave them utterance.
> **Acts 2:1–4**

This was supernatural. They were filled with the Holy Spirit and with fire! They couldn't contain what they were experiencing. They were loud; they staggered out of the Upper Room and into the Temple grounds like drunkards, talking in tongues the whole way! People were drawn to them like a magnet! Those filled with the Spirit didn't know what they were saying because they were speaking in a language they had never learned. But people from other nations heard them speaking in their own language. When they tried to converse with them, they couldn't. Others spoke in a language no one understood. People said they were drunk. Their words seemed slurred like a drunk person. No one understood them.

> And there were dwelling in Jerusalem Jews, devout men, from every nation under heaven. And when this sound occurred, the multitude came together, and were confused, because everyone heard them speak in his own language. Then they were all amazed and marveled, saying to one another, "Look, are not all these who speak Galileans? And how is it that we hear, each in our own language in which we were born? Parthians and Medes and Elamites, those dwelling in Mesopotamia, Judea and Cappadocia, Pontus and Asia, Phrygia and Pamphylia, Egypt and the parts of Libya adjoining Cyrene, visitors from Rome, both Jews and proselytes, Cretans and Arabs – we hear them speaking in our own tongues the wonderful works of God." So they were all amazed and perplexed, saying to one another, "Whatever could this mean?" Others mocking said, "They are full of new wine."
>
> Acts 2:5–13

THE CHURCH

Whatever you may think about speaking in tongues and the baptism of the Holy Spirit, one thing I think we can all agree on: it was supernatural and it caused the people to gather. This was something God was doing by the power of the Holy Spirit. Peter looked at the crowd and heard people talk about them being drunk. That's when he lifted up his voice with new-found power and said, "Drunk? We're not drunk! But this is that which was prophesied . . ." (Acts 2:16) and he began to preach to them. He preached under the direction and unction of the Holy Spirit. He preached a compelling message that revealed Christ to them. Once again, they were convicted of sin. He ended it by saying:

> "Therefore let all the house of Israel know assuredly that God has made this Jesus, whom you crucified, both Lord and Christ." Now when they heard this, they were cut to the heart, and said to Peter and the rest of the apostles, "Men and brethren, what shall we do?" Then Peter said to them, "Repent, and let every one of you be baptized in the name of Jesus Christ for the

> remission of sins; and you shall receive the gift of the Holy Spirit. For the promise is to you and to your children, and to all who are afar off, as many as the Lord our God will call."
>
> Acts 2:36-39

Peter had become a Walking Revival! Christ, by the power of the Holy Spirit, was building His Church through Peter. The Church that Jesus is building has always been and will always be supernatural. Most scholars agree that on the Day of Pentecost, Christ gave birth to His Church in the earth. From that day forward, there has always been a physical Church in the earth. It is a living organism, not an organization. His Church is alive and well.

> And with many other words he testified and exhorted them, saying, "Be saved from this perverse generation." Then those who gladly received his word were baptized; and that day about three thousand souls were added to them. And they continued steadfastly in the apostles' doctrine and fellowship, in the breaking of bread, and in prayers. Then fear came upon every soul, and many wonders and signs were done through the apostles. Now all who believed were together, and had all things in common, and sold their possessions and goods, and divided them among all, as anyone had need. So continuing daily with one accord in the temple, and breaking bread from house to house, they ate their food with gladness and simplicity of heart, praising God and having favor with all the people. And the Lord added to the church daily those who were being saved.
>
> Acts 2:40-47

I believe the Book of Acts ought to be called The Acts of the Holy Spirit, because that's what it is. Look at verse 39 again: "For the promise is to you and to your children, and to all who are afar off, as many as the Lord our God will call." The promise of the Holy Spirit that Jesus gave the disciples wasn't just for them. It was for everyone; in every generation and every nation from the Day of Pentecost until now. The experience they had on the Day of Pentecost was considered normal Christianity from that day on. People gathered together daily and constantly learned. They had a hunger for God that they had never known before. They were experiencing the power of God like never before. His Church is supernatural! Every time I think about how supernatural the Church really is, I think about when Jesus walked on water.

> Immediately Jesus made His disciples get into the boat and go before Him to the other side, while He sent the multitudes away. And when He had sent the multitudes away, He went up on the mountain by Himself to pray. Now when evening came, He was alone there. But the boat was now in the middle of the sea, tossed by the waves, for the wind was contrary. Now in the fourth watch of the night Jesus went to them, walking on the sea. And when the disciples saw Him walking on the sea, they were troubled, saying, "It is a ghost!" And they cried out for fear. But immediately Jesus spoke to them, saying, "Be of good cheer! It is I; do not be afraid." And Peter answered Him and said, "Lord, if it is You, command me to come to You on the water." So He said, "Come." And when Peter had come down out of the boat, he walked on the water to go to Jesus. But when he saw that the wind was boisterous, he was afraid; and beginning to sink he cried out, saying, "Lord, save me!" And immediately Jesus stretched out His hand and caught him, and said to him, "O you of little faith, why did you doubt?" And when they got into the boat, the wind ceased. Then those who were in the boat came and worshiped Him, saying, "Truly You are the Son of God."
> **Matthew 14:22-33**

Once again, Jesus was a Walking Revival. After ministering to the multitudes, He told the disciples (servants) to get into the boat and row to the other side of the sea. They probably asked, "Lord, aren't you coming with us?" and He said, "I'll catch up with you later." The disciples didn't question why He wasn't coming with them at that time, or how He would catch up with them. They simply obeyed Him. They were disciples. As they got into the boat and began to row, Jesus sent the multitudes away and went up on the mountainside alone to pray. As the sun went down and it grew dark, a storm came upon the sea. The wind began to stir the waters. As the storm became more violent, the disciples were rowing and turning the boat into the wind just to keep it from overturning. That certain sense of safety inside a boat is only apparent as long as it is not sinking. Clouds probably blocked out the stars and shrouded all lights on the distant shores from the disciples' view. All was darkness around them. They were no longer rowing to get to the other side; they were rowing just to stay afloat and survive the storm.

Suddenly, in a flash of lightning, they see what they think is a ghost walking toward them on the water and they cry out. Then Jesus immediately speaks to them, "Be of good cheer! It is I; do not be afraid." They were afraid, but Jesus cheers them up. And then – and this will mess with anyone's mind – in the middle of it all, with the storm still raging, Peter opens his mouth and says, "Lord, if it is You, command me to come to You on the water." Suddenly, he had faith – the opposite of the fear that was a moment ago. I don't think I could ever have spoken those words as Peter did under those circumstances. Discipleship was at work in his life. Jesus, the Walking Revival, had made an impact on this simple fisherman. Peter wasn't just blowing smoke to impress his fellow disciples. He really meant what he said. Then Jesus said, "Come."

Faith isn't just saying the right words. It is putting action to your words. And when Peter had come down out of the boat, he walked on the water to go to Jesus. He was literally walking on the water in the midst of a raging sea. I don't think Peter ever thought about doing something like this in his wildest imaginations growing up as a fisherman. He knew how to swim. But who ever thought he would walk on the sea – especially in a dark, raging storm!

It probably never even crossed his mind. And now he wasn't imagining it. He was walking on water! This was supernatural!

This was the power of God at work. As he focused completely on Jesus, he walked on the water. Then he looked around him. "But when he saw that the wind was boisterous, he was afraid; and beginning to sink he cried out, saying, "Lord, save me!" And immediately Jesus stretched out His hand and caught him, and said to him, "O you of little faith, why did you doubt?" He wasn't speaking to the disciples in the boat. He was speaking to Peter individually. Just like God will speak to you and me individually. Faith took action; doubt killed it. Faith brings forth life; doubt and unbelief brings forth death. Almost everything in life can be reduced to a choice between two things, just like Adam's choice in the Garden. As soon as Jesus got in the boat with Peter, the wind ceased.

As I read this story one day, God began speaking to me. He said, "This is the Christian life. It is as supernatural as a person walking on water." Since then I have been firmly convinced that everything we experience in life is God at work in us, causing the Seed of Christ to grow and develop within. Look to Jesus; walk on water. Then those who were in the boat came and worshiped Him, saying, "Truly You are the Son of God."

If you're not saved and don't know Jesus Christ as your personal Savior, this is a perfect time to be saved, right now. Pray a simple prayer acknowledging you are a sinner before God and tell Him you want His forgiveness. Tell Him you're sorry for all your sins (repent) and that you want to be born again. And in the midst of whatever adversity you're facing, He will save you and bring you into the boat. That's when He becomes very real to you and the winds cease and you have His peace that passes all understanding (Philippians 4:7). God will do this for you.

> But what does it say? "The word is near you, in your mouth and in your heart" (that is, the word of faith which we preach): that if you confess with your mouth the Lord Jesus and believe in

your heart that God has raised Him from the dead, you will be saved. For with the heart one believes unto righteousness, and with the mouth confession is made unto salvation. For the Scripture says, "Whoever believes on Him will not be put to shame." For there is no distinction between Jew and Greek, for the same Lord over all is rich to all who call upon Him. For "whoever calls on the name of the LORD shall be saved."
Romans 10:8–13

This is revival! Your own personal revival! This is where Jesus, the Walking Revival, plants His seed within you. Your journey in God begins at this moment. You will never be the same. It is an abundant life that He has for you now, and as you begin to grow in Christ, you will learn how to live daily His resurrection life within!

JESUS PRODUCED WALKING REVIVALS

Jesus is the Chief Walking Revival, the firstborn of many brethren (Romans 8:29). As you search the Scriptures you will find how He brought the reality of God to bear upon a person or a situation, thus causing many to gravitate toward Him in a supernatural way. Over and over again, you will read about the multitudes that followed Him, sat and listened to Him, and were forever changed by Him.

Nicodemus was a godly man even in his generation. As he heard more and more about Jesus, His message and miracles, he came to Jesus one night. Read the story in the first 21 verses of John chapter 3. We know that Nicodemus had a definite experience with Christ that changed His life from the next two times we hear about him in John chapter 7 and chapter 19, at Jesus' trial and at His burial.

> Then the officers came to the chief priests and Pharisees, who said to them, "Why have you not brought Him?" The officers answered, "No man ever spoke like this Man!" Then the Pharisees answered them, "Are you also deceived? Have any of

> the rulers or the Pharisees believed in Him? But this crowd that does not know the law is accursed." Nicodemus (he who came to Jesus by night, being one of them) said to them, "Does our law judge a man before it hears him and knows what he is doing?" They answered and said to him, "Are you also from Galilee? Search and look, for no prophet has arisen out of Galilee." And everyone went to his own house.
> **John 7:45–53**

> After this, Joseph of Arimathea, being a disciple of Jesus, but secretly, for fear of the Jews, asked Pilate that he might take away the body of Jesus; and Pilate gave him permission. So he came and took the body of Jesus. And Nicodemus, who at first came to Jesus by night, also came, bringing a mixture of myrrh and aloes, about a hundred pounds. Then they took the body of Jesus, and bound it in strips of linen with the spices, as the custom of the Jews is to bury. Now in the place where He was crucified there was a garden, and in the garden a new tomb in which no one had yet been laid. So there they laid Jesus, because of the Jews' Preparation Day, for the tomb was nearby.
> **John 19:38–42**

In Luke 7, we read about a funeral procession where Jesus the Walking Revival raised the corpse of a boy from the dead and affected everyone around him.

> Now it happened, the day after, that He went into a city called Nain; and many of His disciples went with Him, and a large crowd. And when He came near the gate of the city, behold, a dead man was being carried out, the only son of his mother; and she was a widow. And a large crowd from the city was with her. When the Lord saw her, He had compassion on her and said to her, "Do not weep." Then He came and touched the open coffin, and those who carried him stood still. And He said, "Young man, I say to you, arise." So he who was dead sat up and began to speak. And He presented him to his mother. Then fear came upon all, and they glorified God, saying, "A great prophet has risen up among us"; and, "God has visited His people."
> **Luke 7:11–16.**

Jesus the Walking Revival had a way of stirring things up on so many levels. Study the 9th chapter of the Gospel of John, where Jesus heals the man blind from birth, and try to figure out how many people were initially touched by this one miracle and how He stirred up so many spiritual leaders of the day. When He raised Lazarus from the dead in John chapter 11, He affected those closest to Him as well as many of their friends and relatives. The Spirit of God moves through people. Jesus is our example. The Spirit of God was moving through Jesus in all that He did in His short life on earth.

Mark chapter 5 tells of the demon-possessed Gadarene man that Jesus set free.

> And when He got into the boat, he who had been demon-possessed begged Him that he might be with Him. However, Jesus did not permit him, but said to him, "Go home to your friends, and tell them what great things the Lord has done for you, and how He has had compassion on you." And he departed and began to proclaim in Decapolis all that Jesus had done for him; and all marveled.
> **Mark 5:18–20**

These are only a few examples. Study the Scriptures and take notes on how many people Jesus affected as a Walking Revival. It will revolutionize your life! John put it this way:

> And there are also many other things that Jesus did, which if they were written one by one, I suppose that even the world itself could not contain the books that would be written. Amen.
> **John 21:25**

Jesus created other Walking Revivals, who created yet others, and He moved through all of them in the Early Church. As you study the Book of Acts, you cannot help but see this powerful truth at work through believers as Christ builds His Church. There is Peter's great sermon on the Day of Pentecost in which the Holy Spirit transformed the lives of 3,000 people and brought them into the Kingdom of God. Peter and John, the Walking Revivals, pray for the crippled man at the gate called Beautiful in Acts chapter 3.

> Then Peter said, "Silver and gold I do not have, but what I do have I give you: In the name of Jesus Christ of Nazareth, rise up and walk." And he took him by the right hand and lifted him up, and immediately his feet and ankle bones received strength. So he, leaping up, stood and walked and entered the temple with them – walking, leaping, and praising God. And all the people saw him walking and praising God. Then they knew that it was he who sat begging alms at the Beautiful Gate of the temple; and they were filled with wonder and amazement at what had happened to him.
> **Acts 3:6–10**

The man was healed and those who prayed for him were arrested. There was a trial. Peter preached again. That is revival! We see the result of Christ moving through Peter and the Bible says, "However, many of those who heard the word believed; and the number of the men came to be about five thousand" (Acts 4:4). That was just the men who got saved. When you add up their wives and children, you begin realizing the power of this one miracle; how it affected so many people, bringing them into right relationship with God. The leaders conducting the court trial didn't know what to do with the disciples or with the man who was healed. Once let go, the Church prayed for boldness and they were all filled with the Holy Spirit! This is revival! This is the effect of Christ building His Church through people.

> So they called them and commanded them not to speak at all nor teach in the name of Jesus. But Peter and John answered and said to them, "Whether it is right in the sight of God to listen to you more than to God, you judge. For we cannot but speak the things which we have seen and heard." So when they had further

threatened them, they let them go, finding no way of punishing them, because of the people, since they all glorified God for what had been done. For the man was over forty years old on whom this miracle of healing had been performed.
Acts 4:18–22

"For truly against Your holy Servant Jesus, whom You anointed, both Herod and Pontius Pilate, with the Gentiles and the people of Israel, were gathered together to do whatever Your hand and Your purpose determined before to be done. Now, Lord, look on their threats, and grant to Your servants that with all boldness they may speak Your word, by stretching out Your hand to heal, and that signs and wonders may be done through the name of Your holy Servant Jesus." And when they had prayed, the place where they were assembled together was shaken; and they were all filled with the Holy Spirit, and they spoke the word of God with boldness.
Acts 4:27–31

This is Bible Christianity! It wasn't just for way back then; it wasn't just to fill pages in the Bible. Jesus died and rose again to give us relationship, not religion! Study your way through the Book of Acts and find all the Walking Revivals documented there. Let God speak to you and empower you through the Holy Spirit to do the same today!

A HISTORY OF WALKING REVIVALS

Being saved in the Jesus People Movement, which was a God-sent revival, I have always been a student of other revivals throughout history. We read about Martin Luther in Germany during the 16th century, the monk who was converted to Christ and ended up starting the Reformation movement. Out of that also came the Lutheran Church which remains throughout the world today. He changed history in the Western world for the better. He was a Walking Revival!

John and Charles Wesley lived in the 18th century in the United Kingdom. They changed history and out of that move of God came the Methodist movement. You can go to just about any nation in the world and find Methodist churches. They were Walking Revivals! William Booth was also active in the U.K. during the 19th century. God used him to start the Salvation Army movement that changed world history. He was a Walking Revival that produced many other Walking Revivals!

In America we had the Great Awakening of 1734-1743. In Northampton, Massachusetts, a young Jonathan Edwards was pastoring. He reported five or six people converted – one young woman after months of fruitless labor. He was afraid her conversion would destroy what God had begun to do. But the opposite took place. God used that woman. Three hundred souls were converted in six months – in a town of only 1,100 people! The news of this spread like wildfire, and similar revivals broke out in more than 100 towns. He was a Walking Revival and so was his convert, the young woman!

You can read about George Whitfield's dramatic preaching in Philadelphia in 1739. It was as if God breathed upon a fire already started in the Great Awakening. An estimated 80% of America's 900,000 colonists at that time personally heard Whitfield preach. He became America's first celebrity. Benjamin Franklin said he went out to a field to hear George Whitfield preach because he liked to "watch the fire burn." George Whitfield was a Walking Revival!

The Second Great Awakening came to this country from 1800-1840. At the beginning of this revival they say only one in fifteen of the over 5 million people in America went to an Evangelical church. James McGready was a Presbyterian minister who experienced spiritual manifestations in Logan County, Kentucky. He presided over camp meeting revivals and drew thousands from as far away as Ohio. He was a Walking Revival!

Charles Finney began his ministry in 1824 which would eventually convert 500,000 people to Christ. In Rochester, New York in 1831 alone, 100,000 were converted – causing the revival to spread to over 1,500 towns. He was a Walking Revival!

During the Businessmen's Revival of 1857-1858, Jeremiah Lanphier was given a room in the North Dutch Church of New York City for one hour every Tuesday at noon for a prayer meeting. The first meeting was on September 23, three weeks before the Bank Panic of 1857. Six attended that first week; then 20 the next; and then 40. Then they began having daily prayer meetings. One young businessman from Philadelphia who was at that first prayer meeting went home to start a similar prayer meeting. Thousands were converted to Christ there. Other churches began opening up prayer meetings; they eventually spread across America and throughout the world. An estimated 1,000,000 people were added to the churches and as many as one million of the four million existing church members were also converted to Christ. All as a result of Christ building His Church through people.

An estimated 300,000 soldiers were converted to Christ during the Civil War in America, evenly divided between the Southern and Northern Armies. There were many Walking Revivals throughout this period of time in America!

And do not to forget the young businessman named Dwight L. Moody who had participated in the Great Revival of 1857 as it swept Chicago. Moody later conducted revivals throughout the British Isles, speaking to more than 2,500,000 people. He was a Walking Revival!

There was the Welsh Revival of 1904-1905 where Evan Roberts stood behind a pulpit as multitudes supernaturally gathered to repent of their sins. People came from all over the world. Two Welsh brothers, Stephen and George Jeffreys, were responsible for starting over 450 churches in the U.K. during their lifetimes, most of which exist to this day. They say it was common for Stephen Jeffreys to begin a revival service in a rented hall with 25 people on a Monday night and have more than 5,000 people by Friday. When I first began preaching in the U.K. in the late 1980s, I would often run into very old Christians and I would always ask them, "Who's the most powerful preacher you have ever heard?" Every one of them without hesitation would say, "Stephen Jeffreys." These men were Walking Revivals!

America also had the Azusa Street Revival of 1906. William J. Seymour was an African-American Holiness pastor who was blind in one eye. He went to Los Angeles seeking a pastorate. But after he preached his first message, they locked the doors and wouldn't let him preach a second service! He began prayer meetings in a home nearby where the Spirit of God began to be poured out. Multitudes began to come from everywhere. They ended up acquiring a dilapidated Methodist church at 312 Azusa Street, where daily meetings continued for three years. Out of this came the Pentecostal Movement and then later the Charismatic Movement. Many Walking Revivals were birthed in these movements.

After World War II came the Latter Rain Revival and the Healing Revivals of the 1950s with evangelists the likes of A. A. Allen, Oral Roberts, and Jack Cole. These were all Walking Revivals!

The most famous of all evangelists during the last half of the 20th century was Dr. Billy Graham. He was responsible for making Evangelical Christianity popular for a new generation, exploding on the scene during his Los Angeles crusade of 1949. An estimated 180,000,000 people attended his nearly 400 crusades over his lifetime. You can multiply that by the millions who watched his crusades on television. He was definitely a Walking Revival!

The Jesus People Movement of the 1970s simply took the Bible at face value and a lost generation of young people found Jesus Christ as their personal Savior. I was one of them. There were a multitude of Walking Revivals produced during this revival.

The list goes on and on. Study these sovereign moves of God throughout history and learn from them. Allow them to stir your heart to seek after God so that you also can become a Walking Revival. Pray and read God's Word daily to be full of faith and allow Christ to be formed in you and He will build His Church through you. Remember to join yourself to other believers who are doing the same. Real Christian outreach is people reaching people by the Spirit of God moving through them, which will bring those people back into a right relationship with the living God that Adam once enjoyed.

> Now in those days, when the number of the disciples was multiplying, there arose a complaint against the Hebrews by the Hellenists, because their widows were neglected in the daily distribution. Then the twelve summoned the multitude of the disciples and said, "It is not desirable that we should leave the word of God and serve tables. Therefore, brethren, seek out from among you seven men of good reputation, full of the Holy Spirit and wisdom, whom we may appoint over this business; but we will give ourselves continually to prayer and to the ministry of the word." And the saying pleased the whole multitude. And they chose Stephen, a man full of faith and the Holy Spirit, and Philip, Prochorus, Nicanor, Timon, Parmenas, and Nicolas, a proselyte from Antioch, whom they set before the apostles; and when they had prayed, they laid hands on them. Then the word of God spread, and the number of the disciples multiplied greatly in Jerusalem, and a great many of the priests were obedient to the faith.
> **Acts 6:1–7**

Anytime God moves amongst a people you will find disciples. It all comes back to relationship with God. You cannot give it if you do not have it. Seek God personally; get to know Him. Serving and being a servant is a great thing. But, becoming His friend because He says so, is where I believe God wants every one of us to be. This is a place of faith, of rest. We're called believers for a reason. Believers are branches on the Vine. The life of God flows through Jesus to you and through you to others.

Whatever trial, tribulation or suffering you may go through remember, it is God at work in your life bringing you to this place of friendship. Do you want to be God's friend? Do you want Him to use your life in a powerful way? Then allow God to prune you.

> "I am the true vine, and My Father is the vinedresser. Every branch in Me that does not bear fruit He takes away; and every branch that bears fruit He prunes, that it may bear more fruit. You are already clean because of the word which I have spoken to you. Abide in Me, and I in you. As the branch cannot bear fruit of itself, unless it abides in the vine, neither can you, unless you abide in Me."
> **John 15:1-4**

It is God's pruning process that causes us to bear fruit that remains. Every once in a while, I run across someone who tells me they are praying for God to humble them. I tell them not to pray like that anymore because the Bible says we're to humble ourselves.

> Likewise you younger people, submit yourselves to your elders. Yes, all of you be submissive to one another, and be clothed with humility, for "God resists the proud, but gives grace to the humble." Therefore humble yourselves under the mighty hand of God, that He may exalt you in due time, casting all your care upon Him, for He cares for you. Be sober, be vigilant; because your adversary the devil walks about like a roaring lion, seeking whom he may devour. Resist him, steadfast in the faith, knowing that the same sufferings are experienced by your brotherhood in

the world. But may the God of all grace, who called us to His eternal glory by Christ Jesus, after you have suffered a while, perfect, establish, strengthen, and settle you. To Him be the glory and the dominion forever and ever. Amen.
1 Peter 5:5–11

From the moment we give our lives to Jesus, we are grafted into the Vine. His life begins flowing through our life. We need to live our lives from God's perspective on sufferings and trials. Live Christ daily and He will help you to get closer to Himself. This is revival. Your own personal revival. There is no telling what God can do through this relationship you are building with Him.

> Beloved, do not think it strange concerning the fiery trial which is to try you, as though some strange thing happened to you; but rejoice to the extent that you partake of Christ's sufferings, that when His glory is revealed, you may also be glad with exceeding joy. If you are reproached for the name of Christ, blessed are you, for the Spirit of glory and of God rests upon you.
> **1 Peter 4:12–14**

This was the revelation the Early Church walked in. The apostles had it. They passed it on to disciples in the Church. Paul especially lived it.

> But what things were gain to me, these I have counted loss for Christ. Yet indeed I also count all things loss for the excellence of the knowledge of Christ Jesus my Lord, for whom I have suffered the loss of all things, and count them as rubbish, that I may gain Christ and be found in Him, not having my own righteousness, which is from the law, but that which is through faith in Christ, the righteousness which is from God by faith; that I may know Him and the power of His resurrection, and the fellowship of His sufferings, being conformed to His death, if, by any means, I may attain to the resurrection from the dead.
> **Philippians 3:7–11**

Do you really want revival? People ask me all the time, "Do you believe there's going to be an end-time revival?" I tell them, "Yes, I do. It starts with you." If you are willing to suffer loss for Christ, you are in a good place for God to move through you to reach the world. I believe in the Last Days we're going to see more and more Walking Revivals! Are you one of them? Do you want to be? Get to genuinely know God and allow His life to flow through you.

> And we know that all things work together for good to those who love God, to those who are the called according to His purpose.
> **Romans 8:28**

CHAPTER NINE

REALITY

Being confident of this very thing, that He who has begun a good work in you will complete it until the day of Jesus Christ.
Philippians 1:6

LARRY REED

There is one Walking Revival who stands out to me because, not only did I personally know him, but his influence in my life and on thousands of others around the world is legendary. His name is Larry Reed. When God began opening my eyes to the thought of such a thing as a Walking Revival, it was Larry Reed who was constantly at the forefront of those thoughts. I've never known anyone like him.

To give you the significance of the impact that this man of God had, I need to give you a bit of a history lesson – compiled from my own personal, first-hand experiences as well as my understanding of events leading up to the Jesus People Movement. Putting it all together has been quite revealing as to how extensively God may use a Walking Revival for His purposes.

Let's begin with Pennsylvania Pastor David Wilkerson, directed to New York City by the Spirit of God in 1958 to try and help teenage members of a Puerto Rican gang called the Egyptian Kings who were on trial there for murder. The gang had gone to Highbridge Park in New York City and killed a 15-year-old polio victim named Michael Farmer. Wilkerson entered the courtroom and asked the judge for permission to speak to the gang. He was thrown out. A picture of the preacher holding up his Bible in the courtroom was all over the newspapers the next day. Thus began the country preacher's ministry in the big city of New York through which addicts, gang members, and drug dealers would be consumed by the Word of God instead of being destroyed by the streets of the city. The story of gang member Nicky Cruz's conversion is told in Wilkerson's best-selling book, *The Cross and the Switchblade*, first published in 1963. (The film adaptation was released in 1970.) Mau Mau members Nicky Cruz and Israel Narvaez both became Christians under Wilkerson's ministry. I've heard them both preach and minister. Nicky Cruz later became an evangelist himself and wrote the autobiographical *Run Baby Run*. By 1967 David Wilkerson, a real Walking Revival, traveled the country by car preaching youth crusades. He had an evangelistic ministry aimed at middle-class youth who were restless and bored. His goal was to prevent them from becoming heavily involved with drugs, alcohol, or violence. I believe this ministry laid the groundwork in the youth of America for what God was about to do during the Jesus People Movement a few years later.

In 1958, David Wilkerson founded Teen Challenge, an Evangelical Christian addiction recovery program, in Brooklyn. The first young drug addict to come out of Teen Challenge successfully was Sonny Arguinzoni. He moved to La Puente, California to attend the Latin American Bible College where he met his future wife, Julie. After marrying, the couple moved to Los Angeles and started a church in their home. In 1967, Pastor Sonny and Julie founded Victory Outreach in a small building in the Boyle Heights neighborhood of East Los Angeles. But after a few years Sonny called Wilkerson to let him know they were about to call it quits, as they couldn't grow beyond 25 people. He told Wilkerson he had scheduled a series of revival meetings with a Foursquare evangelist a friend had told him about. So when John Metzler went to the small church to hold a few meetings, neither he nor Sonny had any idea what God was about to do.

The meetings lasted for more than three weeks and over 750 people got radically saved! Many of them were drug addicts and gang members who were miraculously set free from addiction. John Metzler was a Walking Revival! He had prior commitments and had to leave, but when he returned three months later, another 750 were saved. Sonny was now running 1,500 plus people in his church and he never looked back. God did this! It was the work of His grace. He was moving through people to build His Church.

Larry Reed was a drug addict. Addicted to heroin from the first moment he put a needle in his arm. To support his habit he lived a life of crime. He was arrested many times and wound up in San Quentin Prison. An hour after getting out of prison, he was already sticking a needle in his arm to get high again. "Once a drug addict, always a drug addict," they told him. He did his second stint in San Quentin for armed robbery. He had pulled a gun on a little boy, ready to kill him just to get some money for one more fix.

At his parole hearing, he conned the board into believing he had become a Christian. They put him on parole in a Christian halfway house. One of the young directors of that halfway house was Andrae Crouch, whose father pastored a large black Pentecostal church. Andrae was street-wise to the cons. He had experience. So here was Larry, playing the con, acting like a Christian, but breaking all rules of the house every chance he got. One day, they finally had enough and kicked him out of the halfway house. They said there was no hope for him. Once a drug addict, always a drug addict. Once a con, always a con.

So Larry sat on the front lawn of the house for more than four hours. He wouldn't leave, no matter how many times they told him to hit the road. As he explains in his testimony, "If I was to step foot on that sidewalk, I will be officially AWOL, and the parole officer would pick me up and I would end up having to do the rest of my time in San Quentin. I didn't want that." He just sat there crying and begging them for one more chance. So they did. They told him he would have to obey all the rules, and couldn't mess up once, or they would call the parole officer to come pick him up.

That night they told Larry and the other guys they were all going to church. They packed them in a van and went to Sonny Arguinzoni's church, arriving early for prayer meeting. In his testimony Larry tells about entering the prayer room at church and seeing about twenty guys in a big circle, holding hands. Some of them he had shot drugs with. Others he had done time in prison with. And they were holding hands. All he could think was, what a bunch of sissies. What happened to these guys, anyway? Then one of them yelled out, "Hey, Larry! When did you get out? I didn't know you were a Christian! When did you get saved?" He mumbled something incoherent as another dropped the hand next to him, reached out to him and said, "Come join us, brother!" Then Larry said all of a sudden these ex-cons and ex-hypes started speaking in tongues and crying out to Jesus. He just bowed his head and mumbled something, trying to fit in, playing his con game.

Prayer meeting ended and they went into the sanctuary because service was about to begin. Larry sat on the back row, playing his new role. Sonny preached and pulled an altar call for sinners. Four men raised their hands to get saved. Larry had done time with a couple of them. He was amazed to watch them walk to the front to pray. As they did so, Sonny said through the microphone for all to hear, "Larry Reed! Come down to the front and help me pray for these to get saved." He was put on the spot. He had to keep up his new image, so he got up and strolled to the front with his "cool" strut.

He stood behind the four men, not knowing quite what to do. All of a sudden, Sonny stretched his hand out past the four men and laid it on Larry's forehead. Larry immediately fell to the ground, slain by the power of God! He began to speak in other tongues as he lay there for around thirty minutes. Church was over, but Larry told me he was stuck on the ground and couldn't get up for the longest time. Then all at once, he shot up off the floor like a rocket, jumping up and down and yelling, "Hallelujah! He's alive! Jesus is alive! He loves us! He loves me! He loves you!" He started hugging everyone within reach as he continued. He had been converted and filled with the Holy Spirit all at the same time while God had him down on the floor. He got up with a profound conviction that God loved him. God loved Larry Reed! Larry, the con man, redeemed by the blood of Jesus. Changed! Transformed! Never the same any longer. He went straight to the streets that night and began telling anyone who would listen how Jesus had changed his life; how Jesus really loves them and can do the same thing in their life that had happened in his. He was a Walking Revival from that moment on.

> Where is the wise? Where is the scribe? Where is the disputer of this age? Has not God made foolish the wisdom of this world? For since, in the wisdom of God, the world through wisdom did not know God, it pleased God through the foolishness of the message preached to save those who believe. For Jews request a sign, and Greeks seek after wisdom; but we preach Christ crucified, to the Jews a stumbling block and to the Greeks foolishness, but to those who are called, both Jews and Greeks, Christ the power of God and the wisdom of God. 25 Because the foolishness of God is wiser than men, and the weakness of God is stronger than men. For you see your calling, brethren, that not many wise according to the flesh, not many mighty, not many noble, are called. But God has chosen the foolish things of the world to put to shame the wise, and God has chosen the weak things of the world to put to shame the things which are mighty; and the base things of the world and the things which are despised God has chosen, and the things which are not, to bring

to nothing the things that are, that no flesh should glory in His presence.

1 Corinthians 1:20–29

Larry Reed was a radical street preacher when I met him. About three months after I received Christ as Savior, he came to do a revival for our small church. We were running 20 people at the most. He arrived in an old Greyhound bus that was painted white. On the side in large letters it said: *The Army of the Lord.* Painted on the front was the question, *Are you prepared to meet the Lord?* It was painted in reverse so that people driving in front of him could read it in their rear view mirrors. On top he had built a platform. He would drive into a neighborhood, stop the bus, get several people up on that platform to sing and testify, and then he'd preach. He had 15-inch loudspeakers he could set up and blast the entire neighborhood for two or three blocks. It was radical! It was alive!

Within ten minutes time, he would have a small crowd of 30-40 people listening to his testimony. Many would come out to church and get genuinely saved. Every time he came to our church, it would grow. Not just because a few folks had found a new church, but because sinners were getting radically saved and transformed. Every day he would take us out. Many new converts would go who had just been saved in his meetings. We would testify and preach our testimony along with Larry. I call him Larry because he was like a big brother to us. It never crossed our minds that he was twice our age. He wasn't Evangelist Larry, or Pastor Larry; he was just Larry.

Oh, what a time we had! He was greatly anointed by God and people were drawn to him like a magnet. The Spirit of God upon him was infectious. The personality of this con man turned Jesus Person caused everyone within the sound of his voice to want to come and hear more. For over ten years, Larry would come to our church every Fourth of July. Every time he came, our church grew.

During the Jesus People Movement, Andrae Crouch recorded several Christian albums and his songs were sung in churches all over the world. His most famous song, My Tribute, is still sung in churches today. Larry Reed had called Andrae and told him, "I had a dream about you the other night. I dreamed that you were going to write a song that is going to go around the world. It will be the biggest song you've ever written to this day." A couple of years later, Larry was in the hospital because of a serious car accident, and in came Andrae to see him. He told Larry about the song that God gave him, according to the dream that Larry had told him about. Then he began singing it to Larry in the hospital room. You have probably heard the chorus of that song; you may have even sung it time and again in church:

> To God be the glory,
> To God be the glory,
> To God be the glory,
> For the things He has done.
>
> With His blood He has saved me,
> With His power He has raised me,
> To God be the glory,
> For the things He has done.

Larry Reed impacted so many lives that a book could be written just on a collection of Larry Reed stories. I began pastoring in 1977 and Larry Reed came and preached for me in every church I pastored. I have enough stories with him to write a book. I will share one with you so you get the idea of the man who God used to be a Walking Revival.

I was pastoring my first church in Douglas, Arizona. When he came in for me there, he no longer had the big bus. He was driving a little green Ford Pinto. But he had built a rack on top of it for his two large speakers that he kept from the bus. The car looked like a little mouse coming down the street with two big grey ears on top.

He drove around town with a microphone in his hand and preached to anyone in sight. I told Larry about the large park next to the high school where the students went every day to eat lunch; many of them also went there to get high. We went over there during lunch time and Larry drove his Pinto right up onto the grass and into the park. As he got close to a group of students who were smoking up, Larry got on his mic and blasted them. "There's no hope in dope! There's no hope in the Pope! Jesus is the only one who can save you! Jesus loves you! Jesus can set you free!" The students got up and started running away and Larry just laughed.

Later we were going down one of the streets when a couple blocks up ahead a police car turned onto the street and headed our way. Larry slumped down in his seat and said, "Oh, no! It's the MAN! You don't know if he sees us, do you?" And we'd just laugh our heads off in that little green car with the mouse ears.

Larry was bold. He was on fire. Anyone who got around him caught that same boldness and fire. Years later, in 2008, I interviewed him for a video on the occasion of our church's 35th Anniversary. He told me that in those days he had a strategy. He would go on an outreach in the daytime and mostly the women would come out. That night he would jam the men and work on their pride and egos, telling them they shouldn't let the women one-up them. This is how he got the men to come on the outreaches. It worked wherever he went. Our churches were full of men wanting to preach the Gospel and I can think of hundreds of pastors today that were impacted by Larry Reed when they were young converts.

It was common for Larry to be leading an outreach and have the cops show up. As soon as they did he put the mic in someone's hands and told them to keep preaching while he dealt with "the MAN." He was crazy at times. But we had so much fun serving God around him. I've never known anyone else like him. He really was a Walking Revival.

When Larry was a young convert at the dawn of the Jesus People Movement, he had a coffee house in San Francisco, California. "Did any celebrities get saved in that coffee house?" I asked him in that same interview. He casually replied, "Oh, Lonnie Frisbee," before we moved to other topics. Lonnie Frisbee was the young man (who looked like Jesus in the movies) that had met Pastor Chuck Smith, pastor of Calvary Chapel in Costa Mesa, California. It was Lonnie Frisbee that God used to bring thousands of young "Jesus Freaks" into the church. I began to realize that Larry Reed was one of the catalysts for the Jesus People Movement. I don't think he ever realized that himself during his lifetime.

Larry, the con man, was fun to be around. There was never a dull moment. He was bigger than life. And he really loved God. When a person surrenders to God, the Spirit of God moves through them. But God never messes with their personality. He lets us be who we are and just works through that personality. Larry still had elements of the con man demeanor in him, but inside he was a man surrendered to God who knew how to obey. God is after the heart. As we surrender to Him and obey Him, supernatural things will happen through our lives. When the thought of being a Walking Revival first came to my attention, God showed me Larry Reed was an example of what a Walking Revival was all about. In all the years I had the privilege of knowing Larry, he was always the same. He had been all over the world just being Larry Reed, getting people saved and on fire for God. Only heaven will give us an account of the fruit of this one man whom God had saved. He loved God and loved people. What God did through this one crazy man, He can do through you! He really was a Walking Revival!

I AM A WALKING REVIVAL

I can look back through the years and see what God has done through me. I can honestly say He did this and He did that. It wasn't me, but God!

Douglas, Arizona is a border town. At the time I lived there, a small barbed wire fence went right through the city. It was a dying town of about 10,000 people. On the other side of that fence was Agua Prieta, Sonora, Mexico. Neither my wife nor I spoke Spanish, yet Spanish was the dominant language there. About two months after we started pastoring, we were running around 20 people. Every day my wife and I would go downtown and witness to people, reaching out to the community for Jesus.

I had done a lot of fasting and praying for a couple of weeks. At a 10:30 Saturday morning prayer meeting (I was the only one in attendance), I was praying for God to move in this city. As I began waiting on God there was a strong impression in my spirit that said, Spanish Service. Thursday night. I immediately got up off my knees and began pacing the floor, rebuking the devil, because I thought he was mocking me for not speaking Spanish.

After a few minutes, I got around to asking God to move in Douglas once more. Then I got back down on my knees and began to wait upon the Lord. A second time this strong impression hit me, Spanish Service. Thursday night. I jumped up and began pacing the floor, crying out to God because I was confused. Was this the devil mocking me, or just me thinking this up, or was God speaking to me? I really didn't know. As I got down on my knees again this same strong impression hit me. I can't say it was an audible voice, but it was close.

The third time it hit me, I made up my mind it must be God speaking to me, so I simply said, "Okay, God. I believe You're speaking to me to have Spanish Service on Thursday night. I'll need some time to find an interpreter. I need some time to put together a flyer advertising this. I need to get some songs together in Spanish. In about five or six weeks I'll have Spanish Service on Thursday night." And without hesitation, as soon as I spoke this out in prayer, that same strong impression almost shouted at me, NOW! I responded, "Okay, Lord. Spanish Service on Thursday night starting this Thursday night." I went home and shared all of this with my wife.

The next day, in the Sunday morning service, I announced that we were going to start Spanish Services on Thursday night. The whole church began clapping their hands and getting excited. I told them we had no flyers to pass out, that they would have to invite people by word of mouth. After the service ended, I pulled one guy aside who had been saved the second week the church was open. He had been serving God for about two months. Kiko was kind of a shy guy, around 20 years old (I was an ancient 24 at the time), and I asked him if he could translate for me on Thursday night because he spoke better English than the others. He shrugged his shoulders, looked at the ground, and said, "I'll try." I told him I would speak to him on Wednesday night about this. I had never used an interpreter when preaching before.

I then went to Ramón and asked him if he could lead song service on Thursday night. With great enthusiasm he said, "Yes!" Now Ramón had prayed to get saved three weeks earlier as a result of Mellie, his wife, praying for him and my witnessing to him. He was a lady's man. He sang in Mariachi groups nightly across the line in Agua Prieta. Sometimes he didn't come home for two or three nights. He had a good voice, could carry a tune on key, and he loved to be in front of people, singing. To this day I look back and wonder how really saved he was at that time. But he was all that I had. I knew Thursday night would come very quickly. I told him to find some simple choruses in Spanish and that we would use those. "No problem," he said.

After that I went to Carmen, Mellie's sister, who was a senior in high school. I asked her if she could use the high school's mimeograph machine to run off some copies of the Spanish choruses she could get from Ramón. She said she'd try. Wednesday night came. I asked everyone if they were ready and they said yes. They were excited and had been telling their relatives and friends.

The following night, I opened the church building one hour before service, not knowing what was going to happen. To be honest, I didn't expect much. At 6:45 p.m., Carmen showed up with the mimeographed words to the Spanish choruses. I asked Ramón if they were good and he said yes. The words had the chords with them so my wife Susan, who was just learning to play the piano, could go over the songs with Ramón. By 7:00 p.m., people started to show up. By the time we started service at 7:30 p.m., there were 28 adults from Agua Prieta. They had illegally crossed into America to come to church. They had all been Catholic their whole lives and had never set foot in any other church. The fact that they showed up at all was an absolute miracle.

We made it through the song service okay. Ramón could sing and wasn't shy in front of people. But Kiko was another story. When I prepared to preach, I had people open their Bibles to John chapter 3. I was going to preach a simple salvation message because I didn't know what was going to happen that night. I waited a moment while people found John 3 and turned to Kiko and he was in the Old Testament looking for the Gospel of John. I said, "Kiko! You've been in this church for almost three months and you don't know where John chapter 3 is?" He looked up at me and said, "I… I don't know how to read." I replied, "What? Why didn't you tell me?" He said, "Because you never asked." I felt like strangling him right then and there. I grabbed his Bible and opened it to John 3. Then I asked Mellie to read the first eight verses. I preached a simple salvation message and Kiko managed to interpret. I didn't know how accurate he was, but as I finished, I asked anyone who wanted to receive Christ as their Savior to raise their hands. All 28 adults raised their hands. I had them all come forward and repeat a sinner's prayer after me. Shortly after I closed out the service.

Everyone seemed happy and were laughing and talking with one another and with those from my regular congregation. Then it dawned on me. 28 new converts needed teaching immediately. I got their attention and asked who would like a Bible study in their home the next day. A fist fight almost broke out as they argued who should have the Bible study. We finally settled upon one household, and I told the other one I would do one at his house the following night. So Friday and Saturday nights I did a new converts class at their houses. They had others come. In one night's service, a Spanish congregation was birthed. Over the next two months, I did four Bible studies a week in Agua Prieta.

I didn't start or build this church. God did. I simply obeyed the *NOW* of God. None of this had even been in my thoughts before these 28 gave their lives to Jesus. Christ was building His Church. In one service I had a Spanish congregation that was larger than the one I had spent almost three months of prayer and labor building. From that day until today, I still look for the *NOW* of God. I pray for the *NOW* of God. But the story didn't end there. God wasn't finished. He was just getting started.

Three weeks after that first Spanish service, on a Sunday night as we were closing out the service, three women who had been saved that first night showed up and asked if I could go across the line and pray for a little boy that needed healing. Ramón interpreted for me. This little boy was 10 months old and was born with water on the brain and with other complications. He had been in the hospital in Tucson, Arizona since birth and had just been brought home by his parents to die. The doctors gave the boy one week to live. They could do nothing more for the child. The child would go into convulsions about every five minutes and the only way he slept was that they would take him to the local hospital in Agua Prieta to get a shot to sedate him.

I told the women I had to be up at 4:30 the next morning to go to Phoenix for a two-day meeting. We had to make this trip to Agua Prieta quick. After dropping off my wife and young boy at home, I picked up Ramón and the three women and we crossed the border. I have no idea where we went. It was very dark and there were no street lights. We drove on dirt roads because, at that time, most residential streets in Agua Prieta had not been paved.

When we arrived at the house, the door was already open and I could see the living room full of light with several people standing against the back wall. The young parents of the child were there, along with their extended family. Ramón was behind me as I entered. Within a few seconds, I had taken in the scene before me. I saw the people standing and on three walls, I saw Catholic religious pictures. I didn't know that much about Catholicism, but I knew that in Mexico people prayed to these pictures. To my right was a couch with a large pillow on it. On that pillow was the young boy, sedated. Pinned to the pillow was a crucifix.

I immediately turned around and commanded Ramón, as he stepped into the house, to have them remove all the pictures from the walls and take them out of the house. I then commanded him to tell them, "Get that crucifix off the pillow and out of the house!" I use the word command because that's how I spoke to him. At that moment, I surprised myself because I usually don't speak like that; I had a new boldness and authority to speak like I never had before. This wasn't just me. It was the Holy Spirit moving through me at that moment.

When they finished doing what I had demanded, I told Ramón to have them lift their hands and sing the chorus Hallelujah, Hallelujah, Hallelujah, Hallelujah. They had never heard this song before and they had never sung like this before. He led them in the chorus and they sang it through twice. During that time I went over to the little boy, laid hands on him and prayed to God for a miracle of healing. The child didn't move. He was sedated. When I finished praying, I moved to the door as they finished singing the chorus the second time. I told Ramón, "Let's go," and I said goodbye to everyone. Ramón and I went back to Douglas in silence. When I dropped him off at his house, he asked me if God healed the child. I said I didn't know. We'd have to wait and see.

My wife and I left the next morning and returned from our meetings Wednesday afternoon. In church that night, I asked if anyone had heard whether the child had been healed. No one had heard anything. Now, I can't heal anyone, but I know the One Who can. He is the God of miracles and He works miracles today. I figured if no one had heard about the child's welfare, nothing had happened.

The following night blew my mind. Not only were the same 28 adults there, having once again crossed the line illegally, but there were an additional 30 adults in church that night – because God had healed the child. Every one of them were born and raised Catholic. That night they all gave their lives to Jesus and were saved by the power of His might! Our Spanish congregation now had 60-plus adults.

A month and a half later I was in Tucson for a Bible conference at the church I was saved in. I spoke with my pastor, Harold Warner, and told him I either needed someone to move to Douglas who spoke Spanish and could interpret for me, or he needed to send someone to take this group of people and open up a church in Agua Prieta. The next day he chose the latter. Jack Harris, the one who preached the night I got saved, had opened a church in Nogales, Arizona and also in Nogales, Sonora, Mexico. He was going to send a couple from the church in Mexico to start a church in Agua Prieta… and he did.

When the couple arrived in Agua Prieta to start the church, I went with the new pastor looking for a building. We found the old Vietnam Bar building, which was very old and had been closed for a long time. We remodeled it and got it ready for its official opening. The last Spanish service we had in Douglas on Thursday night was awesome. Our small building was packed out and I preached on the Baptism of the Holy Spirit. These new converts were so hungry for God. There was no room to individually pray for each one, so I prayed one prayer for all. Suddenly, the whole place erupted in praise and adoration for the Lord Jesus Christ! They all began speaking in tongues as the Spirit gave utterance. This praise went on for some time and it even looked like there was a bright mist in the room. I've never seen anything like it before or since.

The next night was a Friday night. It was the official opening night for the new church in Agua Prieta. There were 125 people in service that night and even more the next night. I was there. These adult converts had brought their kids and others besides. Jesus was building His Church! The new pastor had walked into a powerful move of God. He had done nothing for this to happen. God did this! The only thing I did was to obey the *NOW* of God. The church continued to grow and never looked back. They had new disciples and the disciples were multiplying as the church grew. Within a few years the Agua Prieta church sent out men and their families to start new churches.

Out of the initial 28 adults who got saved that first night, seven of the men became ministers of the Gospel in Mexico. God did this. Agua Prieta is a large and thriving church today. Over the years, they have planted many new churches throughout Mexico to the glory of God. I simply obeyed the voice of God and He moved in Douglas and Agua Prieta, building His Church. Without ever understanding what I did in those days, I had been a Walking Revival! God used me. I like the *NOW* of God! I look for it wherever I go and whatever situation I find myself in.

But it didn't all stop there. I went back to my 25-30 believers in Douglas after the two-day opening of the church in Agua Prieta. I pastored there for the next ten months, laboring for God, until He saw fit to move me on to another city to plant a new church and to give the 40-50 person church over to a pastor who could speak Spanish. For me, personally, those were very difficult months. Every service, we had a majority of people who didn't want to be there because "the real revival" was happening across the line in Agua Prieta. God used this time of great trial to train me and teach me for things to come. It was all part of His plan to move in my life in order for there to be more of Him and less of me. Whatever trials you face in life, know it is God working in you, pruning, so He can work through you.

Over the last 45-plus years of ministry, I have seen God move like this over and over again as I simply obeyed the prompting of the Spirit of God in any given situation I found myself in – and God continued building His Church through me. I take no credit for anything that happened over the years in these situations. The results were because God moved. He did this, not me. The only thing I did was obey the prompting of the Spirit of God.

YOU TOO CAN BE A WALKING REVIVAL

I want to share a few final thoughts with you concerning the building of His Church in the Earth, from the Parable of the Talents.

> "For the kingdom of heaven is like a man traveling to a far country, who called his own servants and delivered his goods to

them. And to one he gave five talents, to another two, and to another one, to each according to his own ability; and immediately he went on a journey. Then he who had received the five talents went and traded with them, and made another five talents. And likewise he who had received two gained two more also. But he who had received one went and dug in the ground, and hid his lord's money. After a long time the lord of those servants came and settled accounts with them. "So he who had received five talents came and brought five other talents, saying, 'Lord, you delivered to me five talents; look, I have gained five more talents besides them.' His lord said to him, 'Well done, good and faithful servant; you were faithful over a few things, I will make you ruler over many things. Enter into the joy of your lord.' He also who had received two talents came and said, 'Lord, you delivered to me two talents; look, I have gained two more talents besides them.' His lord said to him, 'Well done, good and faithful servant; you have been faithful over a few things, I will make you ruler over many things. Enter into the joy of your lord.' "Then he who had received the one talent came and said, 'Lord, I knew you to be a hard man, reaping where you have not sown, and gathering where you have not scattered seed. And I was afraid, and went and hid your talent in the ground. Look, there you have what is yours.' "But his lord answered and said to him, 'You wicked and lazy servant, you knew that I reap where I have not sown, and gather where I have not scattered seed. So you ought to have deposited my money with the bankers, and at my coming I would have received back my own with interest. So take the talent from him, and give it to him who has ten talents. 'For to everyone who has, more will be given, and he will have abundance; but from him who does not have, even what he has will be taken away. And cast the unprofitable servant into the outer darkness. There will be weeping and gnashing of teeth.'"

Matthew 25:14–30

Here you have three servants. One with five talents, one with two, and another with one. The first two labored in their own strength and ability and were able to double what talents they had. This was commendable with the Lord. He said to each one, "Well done, good and faithful servant; you were faithful over a few things, I will make you ruler over many things. Enter into the joy of your lord" (verses 21 and 23). If, at the end of your life you receive this same commendation, you have done well.

It is this third servant I want to look at with you for a moment. From the first time I can remember reading this parable, it shook me up. I didn't know why then, or even for years later, until God showed me He was the God of multiplication. Once my eyes were opened to this truth, I could understand His harsh judgment on this last servant. He was called the "wicked and lazy servant" (verse 26). His talent was given to the one who had ten talents. Someone once said, "If you want something done, give it to a busy person." They will simply add the task to their busyness.

God is a God of multiplication. Had this servant put his whole life into his one talent, depending on God to help him, God could have multiplied it to 20, 30, 50 or 100 talents. Why? Because God multiplies. As we yield our lives to Him, He will take our efforts and work His multiplication process through them. Had the unprofitable servant done something – anything – with his one talent, God would have gotten involved and there was no telling what could have been accomplished. Jesus called him wicked and lazy. Then He pronounced judgment upon his life. This is the working of the Kingdom of God.

No matter your shortcomings and flaws, God is bigger still. Just as God did with Larry Reed – taking a con man and using him as He did – He can also use you. What matters is what is on the inside. How surrendered and obedient are you? How willing are you to allow His pruning of your life so that His life can grow and shine through? He will allow your personality to stay intact, as long as He has preeminence in your life. The seed has been planted. Go through this book some more and expand on the teachings found here. Don't be lazy or distracted. Be surrendered and obedient.

I believe the end-game for everyone of us is that God can so move in our lives, we can all become Walking Revivals! I also believe a Last Days revival is coming. Many Walking Revivals will be raised up in the Last Days for the purpose of evangelizing the world. In the last five years I have seen a powerful out-pouring of the Spirit of God upon the churches in India. The nation of India has one quarter of the world's population and I truly believe it is the ripest harvest field the world has ever known. You could also call it a Final Frontier. Jesus said to His disciples, "Do you not say, 'There are still four months and then comes the harvest?' Behold, I say to you, lift up your eyes and look at the fields, for they are already white for harvest!" (John 4:35). Lift up your eyes beyond where you're at with God right now to regions beyond, especially to the ripe fields of India. Lift up your eyes NOW!

Will you also be one of those Walking Revivals? Will you allow the God of multiplication to move through your life in reaching others? God lays this at our feet. He will do what He does, if we'll do what we need to do.

> And this gospel of the kingdom will be preached in all the world
> as a witness to all the nations, and then the end will come.
> **Matthew 24:14**

REALITY

ACKNOWLEDGMENTS

I want to first thank Jesus Christ, my Lord and Savior, for saving me and transforming me to the point where I no longer see myself as just His servant, but I am now called His friend. What He has revealed to me over the years began to flow onto the pages of this book as I obeyed His prompting to write it.

I want to thank my faithful wife of 47 years, Susan, who has stood by my side in all that God has called us to. I also want to thank my pastor of almost 50 years, Harold Warner, my father in the faith who has always been there for me and believed in me.

I want to thank God for all my minister friends, several of whom have read each chapter and have given their input to make this a better book. But beyond that, I appreciate their input in my life over the years (a result of our deepest of friendships with each other). I thank God for Dr. John Gooding, a pastor who has been a balancing influence in my life over the last 46 years. Truer friends can no one have than all of these.

I want to thank God for every person that Susan and I have pastored over the years, for without them God never could have fashioned me into the minister I am today. They endured a lot as I endeavored to grow in Christ. We have many stories together.

Many thanks, as well, to all the friends that I have throughout the world. I cherish our friendship. Just to see your faces or hear your voices means everything to me (Norman Klein being one of these).

I want to thank Michael Hauri, the son of a good friend of mine who was willing to do the book cover for me and did an exceptional job of it. My friendship with people automatically passes down to their children also. Such is the case here.

Finally, I want to thank Sue Maakestad, the wordsmith of our congregation in Tucson. I was writing chapter seven in mid-December of 2022 when I asked her to critique a chapter or two because I had never written before. Before I knew it, she was editing – making it a far better book. I appreciate her encouragement and help.

I am grateful for every one of you.

Made in the USA
Monee, IL
28 April 2023